George Washington
A Timeless Hero

Camelia Sims
Laura Gore

ZANA International
Los Angeles

Photo Credits

All photos are courtesy of the Mount Vernon
Ladies' Association.

ISBN 0-9677456-0-8

http://www.homestead.com/zanas/home.html

Printed in the USA

First ZANA printing, January 2000

For
Emma, Kyle, and Marc

Special thanks to Dr. Frank E. Grizzard Jr.,
Associate Editor of the Papers of
George Washington at the University of Virginia,
for reading the manuscript and making
valuable comments and suggestions.

Chronology of Important Events in Washington's Life

1732 - Birth of George Washington
1743 - Augustine Washington (George's father) dies
1748 - First surveying expedition
1752 - Lawrence Washington (George's half-brother) dies
1752 - Joins the Virginia militia
1754 - Leases Mount Vernon
1758 - Resigns from the militia
1759 - Marries Martha Custis
1759 - Member of the House of Burgesses until 1774
1761 - Inherits Mount Vernon
1774 - Delegate to the First Continental Congress
1775 - Delegate to the Second Continental Congress
1775 - Commander-in-Chief of the Continental Army
1776 - Declaration of Independence
1777 - Bitter winter at Valley Forge
1781 - Wins battle at Yorktown, and the British surrender
1783 - Resigns from the Continental Army
1787 - Elected president of the Constitutional Convention
1789 - Unanimously elected President of the United States
1792 - Unanimously re-elected President of the United States
1793 - Issued Neutrality Proclamation regarding France
1796 - Farewell Address is published
1797 - Retires to private life at Mount Vernon
1798 - Accepts command of Army
1799 - Dies at Mount Vernon at age 67

Contents

Editorial Note: In the eighteenth century, spelling was not standardized. Therefore, to make it easy for readers to understand the quotes in this book, some words are spelled correctly and capitalized according to current standards. Except for those changes, the quotes are exactly as they appear in the original sources.

Part One

George Washington's Early Years

Chapter 1

Early Life

History records the deeds of many American heroes and statesmen, but none can begin to compare with those of George Washington. The man who challenged the world's greatest military power and led the colonies to independence was born in Virginia on February 22, 1732, in a small house on Pope's Creek Plantation in Westmoreland County. Not even his parents could have understood the importance of his birth or what his future would hold.

He came into the world at a time of great discovery and adventure. By the eighteenth century, Virginia had grown from a tiny English settlement called Jamestown to a large, prosperous colony with a population of over 60,000 people. The early settlers were transforming the wilderness and founding new cities.

George's father, Augustine Washington, was a Virginian whose ancestors came from England in 1657. A landowner and manufacturer, Augustine developed furnaces for producing iron, which he exported to England.

Augustine's first wife died, leaving him with two sons, and a daughter who died a few years later. In 1731, Augustine Washington married his second wife Mary Ball, the mother of George Washington. George was the oldest of six children. He had three brothers—Samuel, John Augustine, and Charles—and two sisters—Betsy and Mildred, who died as a baby.

As their family grew, the Washingtons moved into larger homes. For a while they lived in a house on the Hunting Creek land, later known as Mount Vernon. Finally they settled at Ferry Farm, across the Rappahannock River from the town of Fredericksburg. It was there that George's father became ill and died in 1743.

George was only eleven when his father died. It was a tragedy causing him great sadness, as well as hardship. Without enough money for a good formal education, George went to a local school where he learned the basics of reading, writing, math, and land surveying. Had his father lived, he might have gone to school in England like his two older half-brothers.

In Augustine Washington's will, a large part of his properties were left to his oldest son Lawrence. According to the will, George would inherit Ferry Farm when he became twenty-one. Until then his mother was to manage the property.

Not much is known of George's relationship with his father; only the famous myth of the cherry tree remains. According to the myth, George received a hatchet when he was about six years old. One day, while playing in the garden, he used it to chop down a beautiful cherry tree. When his father saw the tree, he asked George what happened. Saying he could not tell a lie, George admitted that he chopped it down. His father forgave him and praised him for telling the truth. This cherry tree myth about George Washington's honesty has been well known for many generations, although there is no evidence it ever happened.

Education

Little is known about George Washington's early education, but many scholars believe math was one of his favorite subjects. He also was inspired by a little book called *The Rules of Civility and Decent Behavior in Company*, which described proper behavior in polite society. In fact, he was so impressed by it that he copied all the rules in his notebook, which still exists today in the Library of Congress. Far from being an exercise in penmanship, according to some scholars, they changed his life, becoming a code of conduct that George Washington adopted in his youth and made part of his character. The Rules laid a foundation for his behavior the rest of his life.

The *Rules of Civility and Decent Behavior in Company* included advice, such as:

- Labor to keep alive in your breast that little spark of celestial fire called conscience.
- Every action done in company, ought to be with some sign of respect, to those that are present.
- Reproach none for the infirmities of nature.
- When a man does all he can though it succeeds not well blame not him that did it.
- Associate yourself with men of good quality if you esteem your own reputation; for 'tis better to be alone than in bad company.
- Let your discourse with men of business be short and comprehensive.
- Show not yourself glad at the misfortune of another through he were your enemy.
- Speak not evil of the absent for it is unjust.
- Undertake not what you cannot perform but be careful to keep your promise.

George Washington never obtained a formal higher education, a fact he always regretted. All his life, he sought to make up for it by learning from others, as well as from books.

In his youth he enjoyed reading Seneca's *Morals* and Joseph Addison's *The Tragedy of Cato*, a popular play whose hero was determined to resist tyranny or die. Over his lifetime, he accumulated a library of 900 books. Washington believed in self-improvement. About one-fourth of the books in his library were about history and politics. The rest were about agriculture, the military, law, geography, travel, or literature. Most of his political ideas came from reading and according to some scholars, from his half-brother Lawrence.

Lawrence and the Fairfax Family

George was six years old when he first met his eldest half-brother Lawrence, home from school in England. A well-educated, sophisticated young man, Lawrence soon became one of George's heroes.

Lawrence was an officer in the American regiment that supported the British attack on Cartagena. Although the military campaign was unsuccessful, Lawrence came home with many exciting war stories. Those stories may have been the beginning of young George's fascination with the military. Lawrence was so impressed with the leader of the British expedition, Admiral Edward Vernon, that he later named his house, Mount Vernon, in his honor.

After their father died, George and Lawrence developed an even closer relationship. Lawrence advised and protected George, who often turned to his brother for guidance and support. He deeply admired his brother and wanted to be just like him.

The same year Augustine Washington died, Lawrence married into one of Virginia's most aristocratic families, the Fairfaxes. His new wife Anne Fairfax was the daughter of Colonel William Fairfax, the cousin of Lord Fairfax—a very rich English landowner and one of Virginia's most influential men. The marriage proved to be a turning point for both brothers.

The Fairfax family lived at Belvoir, a large estate in Northern Virginia, a few miles from Lawrence's smaller estate, Mount Vernon. George often stayed at his brother's house, where he met Colonel Fairfax, who liked him a lot and became a counselor and mentor to him.

At Belvoir, George saw for the first time the sophisticated life of the eighteenth-century English aristocracy. His family had been prosperous, but certainly not rich or aristocratic. George had not grown up with the privileges of the upper classes. The aristocratic Fairfaxes not only fascinated him, they inspired him to set high goals and challenged him to reach his highest potential. Among them, George saw his limitations, both in education and social graces. He set his mind to improve himself.

George paid close attention as Lawrence and the Fairfaxes talked about business, land, society, and politics. He modeled himself after them and learned how to behave in high society. His access to such a prominent family helped him socially and later advanced his career because they linked him with the leaders of Virginia's society.

Age fourteen was another turning point for young George Washington. At Lawrence's suggestion, George made up his mind to become a sailor in the British navy. Although he debated the idea for about a year, his mother refused to let him go. She did not want him to "abandon" her and the family for a profession she considered undesirable. Disappointed, he still obeyed his mother, which is just as well, because had he become a sailor, America and the world might never have heard of George Washington.

First Job

Since he gave up on being a sailor, George chose a new career—surveying. Surveying was a socially prominent profession in the eighteenth century, equal with doctors, attorneys, and clergymen. It was a profitable career because all lands had to be surveyed before they could be sold or before towns could be built. It also was a logical choice for George because he knew how to use his father's survey instruments. He already knew how to accurately run lines, mark boundaries, and measure and map fields.

To gain experience, sixteen-year-old George became an assistant for a survey party, measuring frontier lands for Lord Fairfax. Colonel Fairfax's son, George William Fairfax, a few years older than George, was also in the survey party. The two Georges were good friends, making the trip even more exciting. George Washington looked forward to his first trip in the wilderness. He even kept a journal of his first adventure, which lasted more than a month.

At first, the rugged living conditions on the American frontier were difficult for George. Although not used to luxury, he knew the comforts of civilized life. However, the comforts of home where not available on the frontier. One night in a primitive inn, where his mattress was nothing more than a little straw with no sheets and a worn-out blanket full of vermin (lice and fleas), he slept on the floor. Despite these kinds of hardships, he was adapting and learning to adjust. As the survey party went deeper into the wilderness, they slept in a tent. However, several times the tent blew away with the wind, and they slept without any protection. In the wilderness, George also soon realized that he lacked the skills of a good woodsman.

Many difficult and even near tragic events occurred during the trip. One experience occurred when he and the surveyors were sleeping on straw that caught fire. Fortunately one man suddenly awoke and alerted them before anyone was burned.

Another time, at a trading post, they came upon a war party of about 30 Indians. Fortunately, they did not threaten the surveyors. In fact, George recorded in his journal how the Indians performed a war dance for them, an experience he found totally fascinating. He reported how the Indians made a great fire and sat in a circle around it, and how the best dancer jumped up, as one awakened from sleep, and began running around and jumping in the circle. Then several Indians joined the first dancer, and the musicians began to play.

Regardless of the difficulties, George enjoyed his first journey into the frontier lands. He also learned more about the value of land. A few years later when he joined the military, he came to know the frontier even better.

George Washington was almost eighteen years old when, with Lord Fairfax's help, he was appointed public surveyor for Culpepper County in Virginia. A remarkable appointment for one so young, the new job provided him with a welcome annual income.

Surveying was both profitable and enjoyable to Washington. His services were in demand in Northern Virginia, and he worked hard. One of his jobs was to draw a plat (a plan or map) of the site for the town of Alexandria, Virginia.

Washington saved enough of his earnings to make his first land purchase at age eighteen. Having learned in his youth the importance of owning land, he continued buying land whenever he could afford it for the rest of his life.

Among his many careers in life, Washington was a skilled surveyor first. Although he stopped surveying professionally after he became a soldier, he continued surveying on his own all his life. In fact, up until a few weeks before his death, he was surveying his own lands.

Lawrence's Death

George Washington was twenty years old when he lost the person who had become a second father to him. Lawrence Washington was ill with tuberculosis, a disease that often meant death in the eighteen century.

George had accompanied his brother to Barbados in 1751, hoping the warm climate might help. However, Lawrence died soon after his return home.

The visit to Barbados was George Washington's only trip outside what was to become the continental United States. While there, he contracted a mild form of smallpox, which scarred his face slightly. However, it also immunized him against the disease that killed so many people in the eighteenth century.

Lawrence's early death was another tragic loss for George Washington. His brother had profoundly influenced his character, attitudes, social aptitude, and early political views. As a commanding officer in the military, Lawrence had also influenced Washington's next choice of a career.

Chapter 2

Early Military Adventures

Soon after Lawrence died in 1752, George Washington sought a military appointment. When the governor of Virginia divided the colony into four military districts, he appointed Washington as adjutant of the Southern District. At the young age of twenty-one, he became Major Washington of the Virginia militia.

Major Washington

Serving in the militia fulfilled Washington's dream of following in his brother's footsteps. It also helped his social status, because military rank was well respected in colonial society.

In the eighteenth century, the Virginia militia consisted of local companies of troops organized to defend the colony. In his new job, Washington trained the officers in his district. However, because he didn't have any military experience, he first had to train himself. He bought and read several books on tactics and drilling.

One of Washington's first military missions involved a conflict between Britain and France. Both countries had colonies in North America. However, the French had constructed new forts in the Ohio Valley territory claimed by Britain.

In 1752, Robert Dinwiddie, the Governor of Virginia, wrote a letter to protest the French intrusion into British territory. Ambitious young Major Washington volunteered to take the letter to the commandant of the French forces on the Ohio River. It was a special mission that was considered a great honor.

It also was a dangerous mission, made even more difficult by severe winter weather. The French forces were hundreds of miles away from Virginia, and Washington had to lead people through a huge wilderness of deep forests and no roads.

Preparing for the journey, Washington gathered a small team. The team included an experienced guide, an Indian interpreter, a French interpreter, and men to care for horses and baggage.

During the trip, Washington met with Indians allied with Britain and enlisted their support. He also looked for possible additional sites for British forts and keenly observed the French fortifications in the Ohio Valley.

Washington's party traveled about 500 miles through the wilderness to Fort Le Boeuf, south of Lake Erie. There they delivered Governor Dinwiddie's letter to the French Commandant. Although the French ignored the British demands to leave the Ohio Valley, Washington had accomplished his mission.

Brushes With Death

Washington almost died several times in the Ohio Valley wilderness. Bad weather and deep snow made the horses weak and slow, and Washington realized it would take a long time to return to Virginia. Because it was important for the governor to receive his report as soon as possible, Washington decided to take a shortcut through the woods on foot. The rest of his party continued at a slower pace on the original route. Changing into a frontiersman's skin coat, Washington took his papers, provisions, and a gun, and left with his guide, frontier explorer Christopher Gist.

On the way, Washington and Gist met several Indians allied with the French, one of whom fired at them, but missed. They grabbed the man before he could reload, and detained him until dark, finally allowing him to leave without his gun. Washington and Gist continued walking through the night to be clear of the Indians by morning.

A day later, Washington had a second brush with death when he and Gist reached the Allegheny River. Unexpectedly, the river was not frozen, so they could not walk across it. To get to the other side they built a raft out of tree trunks. Since they had only one hatchet, it took them an entire day to build it. Then while crossing the river, the raft became jammed by big chunks of ice. They were in danger of sinking. Pushing the ice away from the raft, Washington fell into freezing water, ten-feet deep. Only by catching hold of one of the raft logs was he miraculously saved.

Since they could not get the raft to either shore, they abandoned it and made their way to a near island where they spent the night. The river froze during the night, and they were able to walk on the ice to the shore in the morning. Gist suffered frostbite in several fingers, but Washington was not hurt. Thankfully, the rest of the journey was uneventful. Washington returned to Williamsburg successful in his mission.

Pleased with the mission, the governor published Washington's report of the expedition. That publication made George Washington's name known throughout the colonies and in England. It was his first brush with fame.

The French and Indian War

In March 1754, at age twenty-two, Washington advanced to the rank of lieutenant colonel. Soon he became second in command of a military expedition against the French in the Ohio wilderness. His mission was to destroy French forts and defend English colonies against French hostilities. When the colonel of the regiment died, Washington again was promoted, this time to colonel, and he took command of the regiment.

Inexperienced in the art of war, Colonel Washington was defeated in the Ohio Valley, at the hastily built Fort Necessity. Washington's first expedition against the French failed. Britain and France built more settlements and forts in North America. They continued their old conflict for control of the continent. English settlements were located mostly on the Atlantic coast, while the French built further inland. The English feared that the French intended to extend their colonies and keep British colonies on the East Coast.

The disputed area claimed by both countries was the Ohio wilderness, also known as the Ohio Territory. The French and their Indian allies harassed and attacked small English communities on the frontier, burned houses, and massacred families. The war between two powerful European nations for control of North America became known as the French and Indian War. Washington was heavily involved only at the beginning of the conflict, which was won by the British in 1763.

In the fall of 1754, the Governor of Virginia decided to separate the Virginia regiment into smaller independent companies. As a result Washington would be demoted from colonel to captain. Rather than be downgraded, he resigned from the Virginia militia in November 1754. He explained that his decision was not based on "any desire I had to leave the military line. My inclinations are strongly bent to arms."[1] But his pride would not allow such a demotion.

Believing his military career was over, in December 1754, Washington leased Mount Vernon from his brother's widow. He looked forward to staying at home but other events intervened, as they would the rest of his life.

Aide to General Braddock

Soon after resigning from the Virginia militia, Washington learned of a new British military expedition to drive the French out of the Ohio Valley. General Edward Braddock—the leader of the expedition—had come from England to fight the French and finish their ambitions in North America.

In May 1755, Washington joined the British forces as a volunteer aide-de-camp to General Braddock. General Braddock selected Washington for the expedition because of his knowledge of the Ohio wilderness.

Deciding it was an opportunity he could not ignore, Washington delayed his plans to become a gentleman farmer. Serving a British general was a great honor for any colonial officer. Washington wanted to increase his military skills by learning from a professional. He also wanted to form a relationship with someone who might later help further his military career.

As an aide-de-camp to General Braddock, Washington had to overcome many challenges. On the long march to the French fort, he became seriously ill. Instead of going into battle he had to stay behind, because he was too weak to ride a horse. However, because he did not want to miss the battle, soon he rode in a supply wagon and rejoined General Braddock.

General Braddock was defeated in the battle to capture the French-held Fort Duquesne, on July 9, 1755. He also was fatally wounded, along with many officers. Even though he was weak from illness, Washington courageously sprang into action. Riding with the aid of pillows tied to his saddle, he carried out the general's orders.

During the battle, four bullets nearly hit him, and two horses were shot from under him. As rumors of his death spread throughout the colony, Washington wrote his brother, John Augustine Washington, and humorously assured him he was still alive:

> As I have heard since my arrival at this place, a circumstantial account of my death and dying speech, I take this early opportunity of contradicting the first, and of assuring you that I have not, as yet, composed the latter. But by the all powerful dispensations of Providence, I have been protected beyond all human probability; I had 4 bullets through my coat, and two horses shot under me yet escaped unhurt.[2]

After the general died on July 13th, Washington buried him and led survivors to safety. Although it was a huge loss for the British, the battle was a major turning point in Washington's life.

Years later, when the Second Continental Congress considered him for military leadership, Washington was remembered as the hero of the Braddock expedition. His narrow escape from death also left him with a strong belief that God had protected him for a future destiny.

Virginia's Commander-in-Chief

After the Braddock defeat, the governor promoted Washington to colonel of the Virginia Regiment and commander-in-chief of the Virginia forces. In his new position, his mission was to protect Virginia's frontier settlements from Indian raids.

Although the appointment was a good promotion, Washington was never satisfied to continue at the same level for long. He had achieved a colonial militia commission, but what he wanted most was a royal commission from the regular British army, which ranked higher and was much more prestigious.

Commissions in the higher ranks of the regular British army were difficult to obtain, and Washington did not have the right connections to get one.

Deeply disappointed, a sad Washington resigned his position at the end of 1758, after serving in the Virginia militia for five years. During that time, Washington had gained military experience and fame throughout the colonies. His military experience on the American frontier made him well known in the colonies. It laid the foundation for his later military career. However, it would take sixteen years and a revolution for Washington to return to the military career he had enjoyed so much.

Colonial Politics

At the end of his first military career, Washington again followed his brother Lawrence's example and went into Virginia politics. In 1759 he won a seat in the House of Burgesses in Williamsburg, the capital of colonial Virginia. As a Burgess, he served in the Lower House of the Virginia General Assembly. Along with his new career, he began his new private life and married Martha Dandridge Custis.

Washington was not as enthusiastic about being a Burgess as he was being a colonel, but he showed great interest in military matters coming before the Assembly. He continued to correspond with former military officers. They considered him an ally and expected him to exert political influence on their behalf. His sixteen years in the House of Burgesses gave him a valuable political and legislative education. That experience also made him sensitive to the politics of leading a war. This became useful years later when he became the first president of the United States.

Part Two

The Man Behind the Legend

Chapter 3

Washington the Man

George Washington, the all-time superstar hero of America, was a patriot, a courageous military leader, and a true statesman. Washington's remarkable life profoundly impacted the outcome of the American Revolution, as well as the founding of the United States of America.

Much has been written about Washington as a founding father and as the first President of the United States. He is immortalized in literature, in the archives of American history, and by one of the most famous monuments in Washington, DC.

His own words reveal a complex and intriguing person—a truly ethical man who did not seek personal gain, but who made many personal sacrifices to ensure the safe development of his country. But do we really understand or appreciate the man whose face is on the dollar bill?

Washington the man, his interests, and his family life are often overshadowed by the historical Washington. Yet it was the totality of the man—his characteristics, interests, character, views, faith, family, and friends—that made him a great hero. His beliefs established his values, formed his attitudes and motives, and produced his behavior.

Physical Characteristics

George Washington was an impressive six-feet-two-inches tall. Although not described as handsome, people found him to be quite distinguished. Washington was physically strong, imposing, yet graceful. Describing his own strength he once said, "I have a Constitution hardy enough to encounter and undergo the most severe trials."[3] The marquis de Chastellux, a French General, described Washington's physique as:

> noble and lofty, he is well built, and exactly proportioned; his physiognomy mild and agreeable...his brow is sometimes marked with thought, but never with worry; in inspiring respect, he inspires confidence, and his smile is always the smile of benevolence.[4]

Unfortunately, he suffered from bad teeth. This problem was first described when he was twenty-eight. Later when his teeth got worse, he wore dentures, which often caused him pain. The false teeth were made of ivory, not wood as some have believed. Unfortunately, dental technology in the eighteenth century was not advanced enough to produce comfortable dentures. His poorly fitting dentures often caused him to close his lips firmly in what appears as an unsmiling, grim look, although he was not really grim at all.

Social Interests

George Washington enjoyed most of the social activities of Virginia's upper classes. He went to concerts, balls, and the theater when he could. He was especially fond of dancing. Even during the Revolutionary War, he found time to dance. In March 1779, General Nathanael Greene on Washington's staff wrote of a dance where his wife, Kitty, and General Washington danced for more than three hours without interruption.

Washington had the aristocratic manners and tastes of a prominent Virginia land owner. He liked to dress fashionably, always elegant in manner. During colonial times he bought his clothes from England, sending specific orders with careful measurements and descriptions of what he wanted. He always preferred to "buy the best."

In 1752, Washington became an apprentice of the Masonic Lodge in Fredericksburg, Virginia. The Masons were a fraternity quite popular among the upper classes in England and America during the eighteenth century. Washington became a Master Mason (full member) in 1753, but refused the higher office of Grand Master in 1778. Although not a very active member, Washington participated in a few Masonic events. In 1778, while in Philadelphia, he joined a public procession to Christ Church to celebrate St. John the Evangelist's Day. That event was also to raise funds for the Masons' charity. In the following years Washington attended more of the St. John the Evangelist's Day events. Later, during his presidency, he took part in the Masonic rites of laying the cornerstone of the Capitol building in the District of Colombia.

As a youth, Washington played cards and gambled moderately. Yet he greatly valued self-control. Later as a military commander, he realized that others were not as disciplined as he was, and warned his troops about the evils of gambling.

Washington also was an outdoors athlete and a superb rider who enjoyed hunting—especially fox hunting. General Chastellux observed that Washington was an excellent and bold horseman, who rode at high speed and leaped over the highest fences. Riding was also a skill very important to him when he joined the military.

Youthful Romances

There are few descriptions about Washington's romantic interests, but from what is known, in his youth he was not popular with the young ladies. None of the ones he liked returned his feelings. For example, when he was sixteen, he wrote of his passion for a girl he described as a "low land beauty," a passion that never came to be. Then he wrote poetry to Frances Alexander, a girl who lived on a plantation near his brother's Mount Vernon estate. She also never returned his interest.

Seventeen-year-old Washington became interested in Mary Cary, and described her as "a very agreeable young lady." She was George Fairfax's young sister-in-law, but nothing came from that friendship either. When he became interested in sixteen-year-old Betsy Fauntleroy of Richmond County, Virginia, she married another man.

Four years later, the twenty-four-year-old Washington made a trip to Boston to see the governor of Massachusetts on military business. On the way, he stayed with a friend in New York and became interested in his friend's sister-in-law, Mary Philipse. However, she was interested in someone else, and Washington was again disappointed.

Some historians wonder whether Washington was infatuated or in love with Sally Fairfax, the wife of his good friend George William Fairfax. In fact, one of his letters to Sally appears to be romantic in nature and shows infatuation. However, there is no other evidence of a romance, and it is most unlikely they ever had an intimate relationship. The Fairfaxes not only were his friends, they were the people he needed to advance his military career. In his youth they were also crucial to his social standing, something that was important to him. An affair with Sally would have destroyed that. In addition, Washington's lifelong friendship with George and Sally Fairfax also makes an intimate relationship unlikely.

Marriage and Family

In 1758, George Washington began his one and only successful courtship with an amiable young widow named Martha Dandridge Custis. He married her in January 1759. It is difficult to get an up-close look into their marriage, because Martha burned their personal letters before her death. Fortunately, a couple of Washington's letters to his wife survived, and they give some insight into their personal relationship and family.

Martha was born in June 1731, the daughter of a Virginia planter. At age seventeen, she married Colonel Daniel Parke Custis. He died eight years later leaving Martha very wealthy and with two small children: Jacky, age four, and Patsy, age two. When Washington married Martha, he took over management, not only of her one-third of the large Custis estate, but also of the two-thirds left to her children.

Martha was a good wife who brought great happiness to Washington. She was dignified and short of stature—about five-feet tall. Abigail Adams, the wife of the Vice President, described her, then the First Lady, as a friendly and good lady who was always pleasant. Abigail found her to be "one of those unassuming characters which create love and esteem."[5] These also may be characteristics that attracted Washington to her.

George and Martha developed a deep bond and strong devotion to each other. During the Revolutionary War, when Washington was leaving to lead the Continental Army, he wrote her a letter that shows his deep feelings. In his letter, he assures her he would:

> enjoy more real happiness and felicity in one month with you, at home, than I have the most distant prospect of reaping abroad...But, as it has been a kind of destiny that has thrown me upon this service, I shall hope that my undertaking of it is designed to answer

some good purpose....My unhappiness will flow, from the uneasiness I know you will feel at being left alone.[6]

Martha's well being was important to Washington. He wrote his brother John, his stepson Jacky, and Martha's brother-in-law, asking each of them to visit his wife and cheer her up while he was away.

As a stepfather, Washington was often indulgent. He ordered clothes and toys from England for Martha's children. He also felt a moral and a financial responsibility toward them.

Longing for his stepson to have the formal education he never had, Washington hired an English tutor to teach young Jacky at home. Then at age fourteen, Jacky was sent to a private school directed by Reverend Jonathan Boucher. Washington asked the Reverend to keep "a watchful eye on him, as he is a promising boy—the last of his family—and will posses a very large fortune; add to this my anxiety to make him fit for more useful purposes, than a horse racer etc." [7]

Unfortunately, Jacky did not like to study, and he became a disappointment to Washington. In May 1773, Washington enrolled his unenthusiastic stepson in King's College, now Columbia University in New York. He did not stay long. When his sister Patsy Custis died from epilepsy at age seventeen, Jacky used the tragedy as an excuse to drop out of school. He never returned to college, saying his absence was too hard on his mother. In February 1774, Jacky married Nelly Calvert of Baltimore.

Two years after his marriage, Jacky expressed gratitude to Washington for all his troubles and efforts to be a good stepfather:

I am extremely desirous...to return you thanks for your parental care which on all occasions you have shown for me...Few have experienced such care and attention from real parents as I have done. He best deserves the name of father who acts the part of one. [8]

Toward the end of the Revolutionary War, after a life of ease, Jacky Custis joined his stepfather's staff as a volunteer aide. Tragically, he became ill during the Yorktown siege, and died on November 5, 1781, several days before the British surrender. Thus Washington's great military victory was overshadowed by a family tragedy.

After Jacky's death, George and Martha Washington raised the two youngest of Jacky's four children, Nelly and baby George Washington. Nelly Custis became Washington's favorite, but George Washington Parke Custis was too much like his father.

George and Martha Washington with Nelly Custis and George Washington Parke Custis

Relationships with His Mother and Other Relatives

Washington was a generous man, often giving money to his mother, Mary Washington, and needy family members. He considered it his duty to help them as much as possible. For example, Washington gave money to a sick nephew so he could travel to the West Indies to improve his health. Another time, he paid to send two other nephews and a friend's son to school. He also paid his nephew Bushrod Washington's law school tuition, an investment that eventually led to Bushrod becoming an U.S. Supreme Court Justice.

While it is difficult to know how much of an influence Washington's mother had on him, most scholars believe the two of them did not have a warm and close relationship. Although Washington continued to take care of her, records show she often complained about needing money. During the Revolutionary War, she greatly embarrassed him by asking the Virginia legislature for a pension. Washington refused to allow it, writing that as long as one of her children lives, family members, not the government, would take care of her.

Regardless of their strained relationship, Washington appreciated his mother. He spoke briefly of "my revered mother; by whose maternal hand (early deprived of a father) I was led to manhood."[9] Mary Washington died of breast cancer at age eighty-one, during her son's first year as president. After her death, he wrote his sister:

> Awful, and affecting as the death of a parent is, there is consolation in knowing that heaven has spared ours to an age, beyond which few attain, and favored her with the full enjoyment of her mental faculties. [10]

Chapter 4

Character

George Washington was not born to power or great wealth, but was known for his good character and reputation. A self-made man who strived to succeed, he was ambitious in his youth. But it was not just blind ambition that led to his greatness, he was tempered by a life-long respect for duty and careful attention to personal character, reputation, and honor. Washington had his own code of conduct where honesty, justice, duty, truth, and courtesy were followed strictly.

Opinions of His Character

Many who knew Washington left written records about him. Their opinions are important because they were eyewitnesses to his life. They give meaningful insights into his character.

The French General, the marquis de Chastellux, who visited Washington at his army headquarters, wrote of Washington:

> the strongest characteristic of this respectable man is the perfect harmony which reigns between the

physical and moral qualities which compose his personality... Brave without temerity, laborious without ambition, generous without prodigality, noble without pride, virtuous without severity.[11]

Chastellux met General Washington in the seventh year of his command of the Continental Army. He had high praise for the fact that the General had obeyed Congress and had not become a dictator. Chastellux wrote:

> It will be said of him. At the end of a long civil war, he had nothing with which he could reproach himself. If anything can be more marvelous than such a character, it is the unanimity of the public suffrages in his favor. Soldier, magistrate, people, all love and admire him; all speak of him only in terms of affection and veneration.[12]

Another person who knew Washington well was Tobias Lear, his private secretary during his brief retirement and during his presidency. In 1788, after living at Mount Vernon for two years, Lear wrote:

> General Washington is, I believe, almost the only man of an exalted character who does not lose some part of his respectability by an intimate acquaintance....I declare I have never found a single thing that could lessen my respect for him.[13]

Colonel David Humphreys, one of Washington's aides and later one of his secretaries during his presidency, knew Washington even longer than Lear. He knew the real Washington, the man behind the legend. He left this record:

> He had too much magnanimity to feel jealousy.... He did not prefer an opinion on account of its having

originated with himself, nor was its value diminished in his estimation because it had originated with another. When the circumstances were not urgent, he was slow in deliberation, taking time to examine the question in every possible point of light.... But when the circumstances pressed, he was prompt & decisive....He loved truth, and sought it unceasingly & endeavored to regulate all his actions by that standard.[14]

Moral Standards

Washington was known among his contemporaries for his integrity, honesty, and self-discipline. Whether consciously or not, all his life he followed the rules he had copied in his school notebook as a child. He wanted to live a life that could be praised by men of high moral character. In 1776 he wrote "to obtain the applause of deserving men, is a heart felt satisfaction — to merit them, is my highest wish."[15]

Eight years later he wrote a member of the Irish Parliament:

> To stand well in the estimation of good men, and honest patriots...has ever been a favorite wish of mine; and to have obtained by such pursuits as duty to my country, and the rights of mankind...will not be among my smallest felicities.[16]

For Washington, morals related to higher principles of right and wrong and respecting a standard of good behavior. He drew strength from his moral compass. Throughout his life Washington considered integrity and virtue qualities to be desired most, and without which success would be hollow.

He advised one of Martha's young relatives who was beginning a diplomatic career to

> never forget that, without virtue and without integrity the finest talents or the most brilliant accomplishments can never gain the respect or conciliate the esteem of the truly valuable part of mankind.[17]

Two of Washington's letters, written eleven years apart, reveal the high standards he set for himself. In a 1788 letter to his friend Alexander Hamilton, Washington wrote, "I hope I shall always possess firmness and virtue enough to maintain (what I consider the most enviable of all titles), the character of an honest man."[18] In the last year of his life he described himself to another friend, Bryan Fairfax, as someone:

> who always walked on a straight line, and endeavored as far as human frailties, and perhaps strong passions, would enable him, to discharge the relative duties to his Maker and fellow-men, without seeking any indirect or left handed attempts to acquire popularity.[19]

Washington's Temper

Washington did have a temper—a trait he considered a flaw and continuously tried to control. The first mention of it is in a letter from Lord Fairfax to Washington's mother, written when Washington was sixteen years old:

> I wish I could say that he governs his temper. He is subject to attacks of anger, sometimes without just

cause; but as he is a reasonable person, time will curb him of this vice of nature.[20]

Most likely, his mother showed him the letter. Considering that George Washington admired Lord Fairfax, it is likely that the observation would have greatly affected him. In fact, it could be one reason he tried so hard to overcome his problem.

Later as an adult, he admitted to having a bad temper. Although he restrained himself as much as possible, his temper flared once in a while. It could have been a character flaw that ruined him, but it did not happen because he valued self-discipline, and worked hard all his life to control it.

Chapter 5

Friendships

George Washington was a shy and reserved man, not at ease with strangers. Yet in the company of friends and family he enjoyed talking and laughing, not at all what one might expect from the "unsympathetic face" on the dollar bill. Colonel David Humphreys, one of his closest friends, described Washington's nature.

> In society he was always modest; & sometimes so reserved & so silent as to be accused of coldness or want of talents for conversation. With his friends (and it was generally his custom to remain at table in conversation with one or more of them for a considerable time after dinner) he was ever communicative, often animated & not infrequently expressed himself with colloquial eloquence....Grave & majestic as he ordinarily was in his deportment, he occasionally, not only relished wit & humor in others, but displayed no inconsiderable share of them himself.[21]

George Washington had many friends throughout his life. In his youth, he began lifelong friendships with several members of the Fairfax family. His personal physician

Dr. James Craik also was a good friend. So were his brother-in-law Fielding Lewis and Martha's brother-in-law Burwell Bassett.

Perhaps because he did not have children of his own, he formed several friendships with men young enough to be his sons. Among them were David Humphreys, his secretary and aide, and Alexander Hamilton, one of his military aides-de-camp and future secretary of the treasury. To those fortunate enough to be in this category, he also was a good mentor. But perhaps his most beloved friend was the French nobleman, the marquis de Lafayette.

The friendship between Washington and Lafayette began during the Revolutionary War when Lafayette served as one of his major generals. It continued the rest of Washington's life, mostly through letters.

Soon after they met, the nineteen-year-old Lafayette looked to Washington as his mentor, advisor, and friend. Lafayette's father died before his birth. In Washington he found the father he never had. Over time they developed a unique father-son relationship. In his letters, Lafayette often mentioned that relationship when he wrote of Washington's "paternal goodness" and his own "filial love."

In 1784, after the Revolutionary War, Lafayette visited the United States. He described his time at Mount Vernon in a letter to his wife:

> after breakfast the general and I chat together for some time. After having thoroughly discussed the past, the present, and the future, he withdraws to take care of his affairs and gives me things to read that have been written during my absence. Then we come down to dinner and find Mrs. Washington with visitors from the neighborhood. The conversation at the table turns to the events of the war or to anecdotes that we are fond of recalling. After tea we resume our

private conversations and pass the rest of the evening with the family.[22]

Lafayette during his visit to Mount Vernon

More than anywhere else, the real, charming, and warm private side of Washington is found in his letters to his friends. Soon after Lafayette left Mount Vernon, Washington wrote him a moving letter full of emotion rarely expressed. The letter shows Washington's deep friendship with Lafayette.

In the moment of our separation upon the road as I traveled, and every hour since—felt all that love, respect and attachment for you, with which length of years, close connection and your merits, have inspired me. I often asked myself, as our carriages distended, whether that was the last sight, I ever should have of you? And tho' I wished to say no—my fears answered yes.[23]

Washington's affection extended to Lafayette's family. Although he never met Lafayette's wife Adrienne, his letters to her were warm and full of praise. In an April 1784 letter, Washington wrote her:

> The charms of your person, and the beauties of your mind, have a more powerful operation. These Madam, have endeared you to me, and every thing which partakes of your nature will have a claim to my affections. George and Virginia (the offspring of your love), whose names do honor to my country, and to myself, have a double claim and will be the objects of my vows.[24]

Washington treated Lafayette's children as cherished grandchildren. Years later when the French Revolution turned violent, Lafayette escaped from France, but for several years he was held as a political prisoner in Europe. Lafayette's son, named in Washington's honor, came to the United States at that time and stayed with Washington. Young Washington Lafayette was fourteen when he stayed with the Washingtons, both in Philadelphia and at Mount Vernon. A visitor to Mount Vernon in July 1796 said that Washington treated young Lafayette not as a mere guest but as his own child.

Even long after he died, George Washington continued to inspire devotion and loyalty in his friends. For example, in 1824, on an official visit to the United States, the marquis de Lafayette showed his deep respect for his friend when he visited his grave site. Lafayette had been acclaimed everywhere as he traveled across the United States. He enjoyed being among the enthusiastic crowds, which wanted to show their gratitude for his help during the Revolutionary War. Yet at Washington's tomb, he sent his son away and asked to be left alone. Lafayette spent an hour paying his respects to his dear friend.

Chapter 6

Religious Beliefs

During the first part of the eighteenth century, many Christian denominations existed in the American colonies. The major ones included the Anglicans, Presbyterians, Methodists, Baptists, and Congregationalists. The Anglican Church, the official Church of England, was the church of choice for most of America's upper classes.

During colonial times, George Washington was a member of the Anglican Church in Virginia. Although he did not go to church regularly, he attended services about once a month. However, during times of crisis and when he was in cities where churches were more available than in the Virginia countryside, he went more often. In 1762, he was elected as a vestryman for Truro Parish in Fairfax County to help administer the affairs of the parish. Being a vestryman was an indication of his social position, not necessarily of his religious convictions.

Washington was a deeply private man. His faith was kept private during his early life. Later he became more vocal about his beliefs. Throughout his adult life he was convinced his destiny was guided from above. His early religious teachings were most likely responsible for his moral conduct later in life and for teaching him right from wrong.

As he grew older, Washington became more dependent on his faith to help him bear his overwhelming responsibilities. Being a man of action, not a philosopher, Washington valued a practical faith seen in the actions of men. He did not leave any record of philosophical reflections or questions on religious issues. Yet his correspondence gives evidence of his belief in a God who is an active force in human events.

In a 1775 letter to Martha about his new position as commander of the Continental Army, Washington wrote about his reliance on divine protection:

> I shall rely therefore, confidently, on that Providence which has heretofore preserved, and been bountiful to me, not doubting that I shall return safe to you in the fall... But, as it has been a kind of destiny that has thrown me upon this service, I shall hope that my undertaking of it, is designed to answer some good purpose.[25]

Faith During War

His religious beliefs became public during his years as commander-in-chief when Washington made his views known to his men. He often repeated his belief that success for his army, and thus for the Revolutionary War, would only be possible with the help of Divine Providence. He believed that religious men made better soldiers, and he often appealed to his troops to attend religious services regularly.

In 1775 the Continental Congress established army chaplains, who were to be paid twenty dollars a month, a salary equivalent to that of a captain. Although happy to have chaplains, Washington considered the salaries too low to attract good ones and asked Congress for better salaries. Congress agreed and raised the salaries to thirty-three dollars per month. In February 1776, Washington announced there would be one chaplain for every two regiments.

By July 1776, Congress agreed to Washington's request for one chaplain for each regiment, a practice that still exists in the armed forces today.

Washington believed that God was on the side of the colonies during the war with Britain. He urged his soldiers to attend religious services because:

> The blessing and protection of Heaven are at all times necessary but especially so in times of public distress and danger. The General hopes and trusts, that every officer, and man, will endeavor so to live, and act, as becomes a Christian soldier defending the dearest rights and liberties of his country.[26]

In addition to asking his soldiers to regularly attend religious services, Washington ordered them to observe special days of fasting and prayer, as well as thanksgiving days proclaimed by Congress. However, several times during the Revolutionary War, Washington himself ordered special thanksgiving services, without any congressional prompting.

Early in the Revolution, before a battle with the British forces in New York, Washington reminded his men that "to be well prepared for an engagement is, under God (whose divine Aid it behoves us to supplicate) more than one half the battle."[27]

Washington often acknowledged divine help in his army's victories. For example, during the June 1778 Battle of Monmouth in New Jersey, when the odds were against them he snatched victory out of defeat. General Lee, one of his top generals, was in command and the army soon was retreating.

Washington wrote his brother, John Augustine Washington, explaining what happened:

> A retreat however was the fact, be the causes as they may, and the disorder arising from it would have proved fatal to the army had not that bountiful Providence which has never failed us in the hour of distress, enabled me to form a regiment or two (of those that were retreating) in the face of the enemy and under their fire...we drove the enemy back.[28]

After obtaining victory out of what looked like certain defeat, Washington did not brag about or take credit for his accomplishments.

> The hand of Providence has been so conspicuous in all this, that he must be worse than an infidel that lacks faith, and more than wicked, that has not gratitude enough to acknowledge his obligations, but, it will be time enough for me to turn preacher, when my present appointment ceases; and therefore, I shall add no more on the doctrine of Providence.[29]

Another time, responding to an admirer's letter, a humble Washington again did not take credit for the American victory in the Revolutionary War.

> At best, I have only been an instrument in the hands of Providence to effect, with the aid of France, and many virtuous fellow citizens of America, a revolution which is interesting to the liberties of mankind-and to the emancipation of a country which may afford asylum (if we are wise enough to pursue the paths which lead to virtue & patriotism) to the oppressed and needy of the earth.[30]

During the Revolutionary War, the Anglican Church in the United States became known as the Episcopal Church, making many people including George Washington an Episcopalian.

As commander-in-chief and later as president, Washington considered religion essential to public and private morality, as well as to the social order of the new nation.

The President and Religion

As President, Washington freely expressed his views on the role of religion in the lives of Americans and their government. In fact, he dedicated a large part of his first Inaugural Address to the providential origins of the United States:

> it would be peculiarly improper to omit in this first official act, my fervent supplications to that Almighty Being who rules over the universe, who presides in the councils of nations...that his benediction may consecrate to the liberties and happiness of the people of the United States...No people can be bound to acknowledge and adore the invisible hand, which conducts the affairs of men more than the people of the United States. Every step, by which they have advanced to the character of an independent nation, seems to have been distinguished by some token of providential agency.[31]

President Washington attended Saint Paul's Chapel, and sometimes Trinity Church, in New York City. After the nation's capital moved to Philadelphia, he regularly attended Christ Church, and once in a while, Saint Peter's.

The first President of the United States saw his role as protector of religious liberties. Early in his presidency, he wrote a letter to the Methodist Episcopal Church promising "I shall always strive to prove a faithful and impartial patron of genuine, vital religion."[32]

Washington was tolerant of other Christian denominations, an unusual view in the eighteenth century. When he had the chance, he attended churches of different denominations. He also promoted denominational tolerance and applauded it in others, as seen in a letter to the Protestant Episcopal Church:

> On this occasion it would ill become me to conceal the joy I have felt in perceiving the fraternal affection which appears to increase every day among the friends of genuine religion. It affords edifying prospects indeed to see Christians of different denominations dwell together in more charity, and conduct themselves in respect to each other with a more Christian-like spirit than ever they have done in any former age, or in any other nation.[33]

To the United Baptist Churches of Virginia he wrote reassuringly:

> If I could have entertained the slightest apprehension that the Constitution...might possibly endanger the religious rights of any ecclesiastical society, certainly I would never have placed my signature to it; and if I could now conceive that the general government might ever be so administered as to render the liberty of conscience insecure, I beg you will be persuaded that no one would be more zealous than myself to establish effectual barriers against the horrors of spiritual tyranny, and every species of religious persecution.[34]

His religious toleration extended to the Jewish faith, as seen in his 1790 letter to the Hebrew Congregation of New Port, Rhode Island:

> The citizens of the United States of America...possess alike liberty of conscience and immunities of citizenship...For happily the government of the United States, which gives to bigotry no sanction, to persecution no assistance, requires only that they who live under its protection should demean themselves as good citizens....May the children of the stock of Abraham, who dwell in this land, continue to merit and enjoy the good will of the other inhabitants, while every one shall sit in safety under his own vine and fig-tree, and there shall be none to make him afraid.[35]

Although Washington was not one of the giants of the faith, a small incident during his presidency shows a growing commitment to church attendance, one not apparent in his youth. On a Sunday morning when the president's carriage was broken, his secretary sent a note to Chief Justice John Jay asking for a ride. "If Mr. Jay should propose going to church this morning the President would be obliged to him for a seat in his carriage."[36]

Washington believed in an active faith that showed itself in the good character and conduct of a person. Thus he complimented the Quakers (a Christian denomination) for being exemplary and useful citizens. Washington also wrote his views about active faith to the Presbyterian Church:

> While I reiterate the possession of my dependence upon Heaven as the source of all public and private blessings; I will observe that the general prevalence of piety, philanthropy, honesty, industry and economy seems, in the ordinary course of human affairs are particularly necessary for advancing and confirming

the happiness of our country....For no man, who is profligate in his morals, or a bad member of the civil community, can possibly be a true Christian, or a credit to his own religious society.[37]

Washington's famous Farewell Address, written in 1796, was one of his most important legacies to his beloved nation. Its lasting significance is contained in the three main topics he developed—national unity, religion and morality, and foreign relations. Washington expressed the need for religion and morality in government and saw it as necessary for the well being of America's population and government.

Of all the dispositions and habits, which lead to political prosperity, religion and morality are indispensable supports...reason and experience both forbid us to expect, that national morality can prevail in exclusion of religious principle.[38]

Chapter 7

Views and Advice

Washington's views can be found in numerous letters and written statements. He wrote on many subjects, including education, love and marriage, and the keys to success.

Education

Washington was primarily a self-taught man, but he had great respect for formal education. Believing his own education to be "defective," he thought nothing was more important to the nation than educating its youth.

He considered "the best means of forming a manly, virtuous and happy people, will be found in the right education of youth. Without this foundation, every other means, in my opinion, must fail."[39]

Washington believed that education was essential to the new nation's prosperity. That is why he asked the Senate and the House of Representatives to promote the teaching of science and literature. He wanted the United States to "cultivate literature and useful knowledge, for the purpose of qualifying the rising generations for patrons of good government, virtue and happiness."[40]

During his presidency he repeatedly asked Congress to establish a national university. In his last address to Congress in December 1796, Washington again asked for a national university to educate youth in the science of government.

As in all things, Washington practiced what he preached. His commitment to education took the practical form of giving money to educational institutions. He also paid to educate relatives and the children of friends. In his will, Washington left $4,000, a large amount of money at that time, to the Alexandria Academy for educating orphans and poor children.

After his brother Samuel died in 1781, Washington took charge of his two young sons' education. Washington took an active interest in every aspect of their education and wrote their tutor "it is my wish that their morals as well as educations may be attended to."[41] In the eighteenth century, dancing was an important social asset, so Washington sent his nephews to dancing school. Because he regretted not being able to speak a foreign language, he directed them to learn French.

In 1783 he wrote to Bushrod, another nephew and the future owner of Mount Vernon:

> it is not the mere study of the law, but to become eminent in the profession of it which is to yield honor and profit; the first was your choice, let the second be your ambition, and that dissipation is incompatible with both.[42]

Love and Marriage

It may surprise some people that George Washington, the father of his country, gave advice on love and marriage. However, the patriarch of the nation was not a busybody matchmaker. Quite the opposite, as he explained in a letter, throughout his life he never tried to promote or prevent a matrimonial bond. Rather, he explained his views on marriage to those he cared about. In a letter to his good friend Burwell Bassett, he wrote "I have always considered marriage as the most interesting event of ones life. The foundation of happiness or misery."[43]

In another letter he wrote, "in my estimation more permanent and genuine happiness is to be found in the sequestered walks of connubial life, than in the giddy rounds of promiscuous pleasure, or the more tumultuous and imposing scenes of successful ambition."[44]

Most of Washington's advice about love is contained in three letters to young women from his wife's side of the family. As patriarch of his family, he felt it was his duty to advise younger generations. Above all, in choosing a good husband, Washington strongly advised the use of prudence and reason. He believed only men of good character and good sense would make good husbands for the women in his family.

Washington's first letter focused on the possible remarriage of his stepson's widow, Eleanor. The other two letters were written more than ten years later to two of her daughters (his step-granddaughters). Eleanor, Jacky Custis's young widow with four small children, was advised "to make a prudent choice." Washington suggested she carefully consider the following in her selection process:

> the family and connections of the man, his fortune (which is not the most essential in my eye), the line of conduct he has observed, and disposition and frame of his mind. You should consider, what prospect there is of his proving kind and affectionate to you; just, generous and attentive to your children; and, how far his connections will be agreeable to you.[45]

Washington was not a misty-eye romantic. As far as love or marriage was concerned, he was very practical. In his 1794 letter to his eldest step-granddaughter Elizabeth Parke Custis, he wrote:

> Love is a mighty pretty thing; but like all other delicious things, it is cloying; and when the first transports of the passion begins to subside, which it assuredly will do, and yield, oftentimes too late, to more sober reflections, it serves to evince, that love is too dainty a food to live 'upon alone, and ought not to be considered farther than as a necessary ingredient for that matrimonial happiness which results from a combination of causes; none of which are of greater importance, than that the object on whom it is placed, should possess good sense, good dispositions, and the means of supporting you in the way you have been brought up. Such qualifications cannot fail to attract (after marriage) your esteem and regard...Without these, whatever may be your first impressions of the man, they will end in disappointment; for be assured, and experience will convince you, that there is no truth more certain, than that all our enjoyments fall short of our expectations.[46]

Washington's favorite step-granddaughter was Eleanor Parke Custis, known as "Nelly." She was the youngest of his step-granddaughters, who after her father's death was raised mostly by Martha and George Washington. During a visit to her mother's house, Nelly wrote her step-grandfather that she was not interested in any of the young men around her. George Washington, who was at the time the president of the United States, first responded by teasing Nelly about her confidence in her ability to resist falling in love.

Love is said to be an involuntary passion, and it is, therefore, contended that it cannot be resisted....When the fire is beginning to kindle, and your heart growing warm, propound these questions to it. Who is this invader? Have I a competent knowledge of him? Is he a man of good character; a man of sense? For, be assured, a sensible woman can never be happy with a fool. What has been his walk in life? Is he a gambler, a spendthrift, or drunkard? Is his fortune sufficient to maintain me in the manner I have been accustomed to live, and my sisters do live, and is he one to whom my friends can have no reasonable objection?[47]

Washington approved of Eleanor Custis's choice for a new husband—David Stuart, a doctor who became one of his friends and confidant. Nelly's choice, Lawrence Lewis, was a happy surprise because he was one of Washington's favorite nephews. Nelly further pleased her step-grandfather by having her wedding on his 67th birthday. However Elizabeth Parke Custis's unfortunate marriage to Thomas Law, a man about twice her age, ended in divorce in 1810, long after her step-grandfather's death.

Advice on Growing Up and Success in Life

Before becoming President of the United States, Washington took time to write his beloved nephews, wanting so much for them to become successful. He gave his sixteen-year-old orphaned nephew George Steptoe Washington practical advice on how to conduct himself.

You have now arrived to that age when you must quit the trifling amusements of a boy, and assume the more dignified manners of a man....as the first impressions are generally the most lasting, your doings now may mark the leading traits of your character through life. It is therefore, absolutely necessary, if you mean to make any figure upon the stage, that you should take the first steps right.[48]

On becoming successful, Washington advised his namesake to gain all the knowledge he could, which will be useful later in life. In addition to studies, he said the person seeking success should learn to be a hard worker and not waste too much time on amusements.

While Washington expected his nephew to have some fun, he wanted him to choose his amusements wisely. He advised that leisure time should always be spent in company "that is the best kind" in the best place he can afford, because "by this means you will be constantly improving your manners and cultivating your mind while you are relaxing from your books."[49]

Washington spoke from experience, having learned manners and cultivated his mind in the company of the Fairfax family. He advised his nephews to find similar good company.

Washington also reminded young George Steptoe to be careful not to waste money. George Washington was a well-dressed man, yet he cautioned his poorer nephews regarding fashion and clothing for young men. "Decency and cleanliness will always be the first objects in the dress of a judicious and sensible man."[50] He admitted that while some conformity to fashion was necessary, it did not mean that every minor change in fashion must be followed. Washington warned that sensible men will think that a person who is a fashion leader has nothing better than lots of clothes "to recommend him to notice."

To his nephew Bushrod Washington, Washington gave advice about friendships and charity. He challenged Bushrod to be careful about selecting friends because they could either improve him or lead him into disgrace. His advice gives insight into Washington's own feelings on friendship and compassion:

> Be courteous to all, but intimate with few, and let those few be well tried before you give them your confidence; true friendship is a plant of slow growth, and must undergo and withstand the shocks of adversity....Let your heart feel for the affliction, and distresses of everyone, and let your hand give in proportion to your purse; remembering always, the estimation of the widow's mite. But that it is not everyone who asketh, that deserveth charity; all however are worthy of the inquiry, or the deserving may suffer.[51]

Chapter 8

Mount Vernon

In his will, Lawrence Washington said that Mount Vernon would become George Washington's property in the case of the death of his widow, Anne. However, when Anne remarried, she moved away from Mount Vernon, and George Washington leased the home from her. After she died in 1761, Washington became the sole owner of Mount Vernon.

The Plantation

The house Washington inherited from his half-brother was much smaller than the house seen today. Becoming his own architect, Washington enlarged the small house until it became the beautiful mansion of a Virginia gentleman. Mount Vernon was George Washington's pride and joy, as well as his retreat from the world. He enjoyed plantation life, always looking for ways to improve his farms. He became a dedicated farmer who bought and read many books on agriculture.

Starting as a planter, Washington raised mostly tobacco, because it was a cash crop. But tobacco was a labor-intensive and demanding crop that exhausted the soil. Soon, he experimented with other crops, such as wheat.

Washington was an entrepreneur who always looked for ways to increase his income from the plantation. One of his best ventures was the flour mills he built on his property. He sold flour under his own "G. Washington" brand. Although he would be considered rich, his wealth was in land, and he seldom had ready cash at his disposal. As a result, Washington was always in need of cash, sometimes borrowing heavily to meet expenses.

Similar to other Virginia estates of that period, the Mount Vernon mansion had numerous dependencies, such as a kitchen, smoke house, workshops, and stables. Being a plantation owner was similar to managing a small town. Washington had many people working for him and living on the plantation, including carpenters, shoemakers, seamstresses, artisans, coopers, and blacksmiths who made horseshoes and tools. Many of those workers were slaves.

Slavery

During Washington's life, slavery was an accepted part of life in the United States. Like other southern plantation owners, Washington purchased slaves, as well as indentured servants, to work the farms. Indentured servants were people who could not afford to pay for passage across the Atlantic from Europe into America. In return for transportation, they agreed to work several years without pay after arriving in the colonies.

Washington was concerned about his slaves' welfare and provided medical care for them. Although he was known for fairness to his slaves and servants, he expected them to work hard. Before the Revolution, Washington's views about slavery were those of a typical southern planter of his time. In time, he became disillusioned with the system of slavery, believing it not to be the best for agricultural progress. By 1786, Washington came to disapprove of slavery, saying he did not want to ever purchase another slave and wished to see some plan to gradually abolish slavery.

Washington did not separate slave family members by selling them individually. In his will, he forbade the sale or transportation of his slaves out of Virginia because it would separate families. He also said his slaves were to be freed after Martha's death, a very rare act in the eighteenth century. His will further said that old slaves and children without parents were to be clothed and fed by his heirs. The children were to be taught to read and write and given a useful occupation until they reached the age of twenty-five. In freeing his slaves, Washington was ahead of Thomas Jefferson, whose slaves were sold after his death.

Management from Afar

Washington struggled with the fact that public service took him away from Mount Vernon for long periods of time. A large estate needed a good manager. Washington was a hands-on manager and was frustrated for eight years that he was not there to personally supervise estate affairs. While he was leading the Revolutionary War, he asked Lund Washington, a distant cousin, to manage it. Washington wrote many long letters with precise directions for Lund and others about managing Mount Vernon. He insisted that he be sent regular, detailed reports about the farms.

Even though his cousin did his best, absentee management took a toll on Mount Vernon. Although the plantation was designed to pay for itself, as well as provide a salary for Lund and income for Washington, bad crops, inefficiency, as well as the hardships of war, resulted in financial difficulties. There were years the plantation hardly made enough to pay Lund's salary.

Returning from the war, Washington worked hard to make Mount Vernon a profitable plantation again. However, he was home for only five years before he left again to serve as President of the United States. Relatives again managed Mount Vernon, and Washington again wrote long letters directing the affairs of his farms and home from afar.

Part Three

Washington at War

Chapter 9

The American Revolution

The first permanent English settlement in North America began in 1607 at Jamestown, Virginia. After Jamestown was settled, the British colonies had a good relationship with their mother country until the 1760s. Like most colonial systems, the American colonies generally were established to economically benefit their mother country. Yet each colony in the New World developed its own legislative body to govern itself, which gave colonists great freedom.

What ultimately led to the American Revolution began as a complaint over taxation without representation and Britain's interference with colonial self-government. Most of the colonists who fought in the Revolution were British citizens who believed that some of their traditional rights were being violated. They had always paid British taxes, but they believed that through their colonial representatives, they had the most control over what taxes were to be paid. Thus the seeds of revolt took root over a growing resentment about taxes, as well as years of subordinating colonial economic interests.

Stamps and Taxes

The French and Indian War fought in North America and won by the British had been expensive. To help pay for future expenses after the war, the British Parliament passed the Stamp Act in 1765, which taxed legal documents written in the colonies. Such documents included marriage licenses, bills of lading, and diplomas. The Stamp Act was a very unpopular direct tax. Direct taxes are paid by consumers up front and are more visible. Indirect taxes are paid by merchants and later included in retail prices. Because the French and Indian War had benefited the colonies at the crown's expense, the British believed the colonists should shoulder more of a burden for their own maintenance. Yet the colonists saw the tax only as Britain's attempt to reduce their freedom. They complained loudly.

After riots in Boston and boycotts of British goods, the Stamp Act was repealed in 1766. However, one year later the British Parliament passed a new set of laws called the Townshend Acts, which imposed taxes on imported goods. These taxes were particularly annoying to colonists because most of the manufactured goods and all the luxury items in the colonies were imported from England. Import duty taxes had to be paid on such items as paper, glass, and tea. These taxes were customs duties payable at the ports of entry. However, even that indirect form of taxation met colonial opposition. Most of the Townshend Acts were repealed by 1773. Yet, the tax on tea remained.

The Boston Tea Party

The Boston Tea Party was one of the most famous incidents leading up to the Revolutionary War. In December 1773, a group of Bostonians chose an unusual way to protest the tax. They dressed as Indians, boarded three English ships full of tea, and dumped it all in the harbor. That incident became known as the Boston Tea Party. Of course, the British merchants, as well as the government, were outraged. To punish the Massachusetts colony, Parliament passed a series of acts in 1774, known in America as the Intolerable Acts. Under the Acts, the British closed Boston harbor until the city paid for the destroyed tea. The Acts also replaced the Massachusetts assembly with a body appointed by the British. In addition, the British army took over some private buildings for army barracks.

Those were serious punishments for the people of Massachusetts, causing other states to sympathize. In September 1774, twelve of the thirteen colonies (except Georgia) sent delegates to Philadelphia to convene the First Continental Congress. The main goal of the meeting was to assert the colonists' rights as British citizens. They were looking for ways to help Massachusetts, and to develop a united plan of action against British measures. They were not yet looking for independence from Britain. After discussing their grievances, the delegates agreed to break off all trade with Britain until the tax question was resolved. Washington was one of Virginia's delegates to the First Continental Congress. He did not play a prominent role.

The Shot Heard Round the World

As tensions grew in Boston, some colonists began hiding ammunition and preparing to fight the British, if necessary. In April 1775, British troops in search of the weapons fought with the local militia in the villages of Lexington and Concord, Massachusetts. It is unclear whether one of the colonists or the British fired the first shot in Lexington, but it became known as "the shot heard round the world." In fact, it was the first armed conflict in what later became the

Revolutionary War, a war of independence lasting eight and a half years.

Prelude to Taking Command

At the beginning of the conflict with Britain, George Washington was leading a pleasant, quiet life in Virginia. Although he was concerned about the British suppression of American liberties, he was not seeking separation from the mother country, only a resolution for equal rights. By 1769, he began wondering about British intentions and argued for the defense of American freedom. Yet, even then he still favored only an economic boycott of British goods, not war. However, by 1774, he did not see any hope in petitioning the British Parliament and became open to other options, including military action.

Washington went as a delegate from Virginia to both the First and the Second Continental Congresses in Philadelphia. In 1775, he attended the sessions of the Second Continental Congress dressed in his old colonel uniform, perhaps to make his availability for service known. Considering Washington's military experience, it is not surprising he was appointed chairman of several committees on military planning.

When it became clear that war was unavoidable, the Second Continental Congress voted to create a Continental Army and searched for a leader. Although there were other candidates, Washington was considered the best leader for the Continental Army. He was well known by members of the Continental Congress, and respected both for his integrity and for his military reputation gained during the French and Indian War.

On June 15, 1775, Washington was unanimously appointed General and Commander-in-Chief of the Continental Army raised to defend American liberty. He said that he neither sought nor wanted the appointment, but felt that refusing it would have brought dishonor upon himself. Washington accepted the appointment with his characteristic modesty. He thanked the Continental Congress for the honor, and said "I this day declare with the utmost sincerity, I do not think my self equal to the command I am honored with."[52] As proof of his dedication to the American cause, Washington rejected a salary and asked Congress to pay his expenses only. His refusal of a salary was greatly praised throughout the war and long after.

John Adams, the distinguished delegate from Massachusetts, favored Washington as commander of the army. In a letter to his wife Abigail, he explained that Washington's appointment would have a great effect in cementing the union of the colonies.

Commander-in-Chief of the Continental Army

When Washington was named commander-in-chief of the Continental Army, there was no real army for him to command—only the colonial militia around Boston. In July 1775, Washington took charge of a disorganized and untrained colonial force assembled in Massachusetts. The enlisted men were dedicated patriots, but they had little military discipline, not much respect for authority, and some were not physically fit.

That first American army had none of the advantages of a modern, well-trained, and well-armed military force. The soldiers were short-term volunteers who enlisted for a few months, or a year, at a time. They were not trained or familiar with the hardships of war. Although some engaged in frontier fighting with the French and Indians, most were familiar with firearms only through hunting.

Washington's first mission was to train and mold undisciplined men into an effective army. Throughout the war, he repeated the advice he gave to an officer in November 1775—not to require anything unreasonable of the soldiers, but to be a strict disciplinarian and see they complied with requirements.

Washington reminded his officers they were fighting for liberty. He urged them to "Discourage vice in every shape, and impress upon the mind of every man, from the first to the lowest, the importance of the cause, and what it is they are contending for."[53] He taught them self-discipline and sought to build their character, as well as military skill. He gave orders forbidding gambling and counseled them that "At this time of public distress, men may find enough to do in service of their God, and their country, without abandoning themselves to vice and immorality."[54]

In a January 1776 letter to a friend, Washington described his difficulties and frustrations as he wondered about the future.

> I have scarcely emerged from one difficulty before I have plunged into another-how it will end God in his great goodness will direct, I am thankful for his protection to this time. We are told that we shall soon get the army completed, but I have been told so many things which have never come to pass, that I distrust every thing.[55]

In March, annoyed by the problems of building an army, he wrote his brother John Augustine, "that no man perhaps since the first institution of armies ever commanded one under more difficult circumstances than I have done."[56]

The American Revolution began with the goal of recovering the representative form of government the colonies had before the Stamp Act. Yet it soon became clear that settling the disputes with Britain was not possible. Neither was reconciliation.

After many debates, the Continental Congress finally agreed on total separation from England. In one act that changed the course of history, the Congress on July 4, 1776, approved the Declaration of Independence, the official document declaring separation from the mother country. In that single accomplishment of signing a document—considered treason against Britain—fifty-six men, charted an irreversible course, risking their lives, the lives of their families, their positions, and their wealth. Many of them paid a high price.

Of those fifty-six men who signed the Declaration of Independence, five were captured and imprisoned, and nine died during the war. Several lost wives, sons or entire families, including one who lost his 13 children.

Yet not everyone in the colonies wanted to be independent of Britain. Some colonists were loyalists who continued to support Britain and the existing government.

Chapter 10

The Revolutionary War

The war that won American independence is known as the Revolutionary War and as the War of Independence. Both names are correct and refer to the war in which Washington led a colonial army to victory.

The Congress was the civilian authority that declared war, but General Washington was charged with leading the army to victory. As commander-in-chief, General Washington was responsible to Congress and operated under its authority.

Defeats and Victories

From Massachusetts, where the fighting began, the Continental troops moved to New York where they fought on Long Island and were defeated. They fought again, retreated, and then retreated again into New Jersey. Victory still eluded them. To escape the pursuing British army, Washington and his troops crossed the Delaware River into Pennsylvania. For a while, the situation seemed hopeless.

Then on Christmas night 1776, Washington and his troops crossed the frozen Delaware River again for a surprise attack at Trenton, New Jersey. They marched through terrible hail and a snowstorm for nine long miles from the river to the town of Trenton. An unexpected and desperate move, its success turned the tide of the Revolution. After Trenton, and a few days later in Princeton, Washington not only regained control of most of New Jersey, he also brought new hope to the American cause. Trenton was General Washington's first victory after several defeats, saving his military reputation, as well as boosting the spirits of the troops.

Washington's legendary courage in battle greatly inspired his troops. He changed potentially disastrous situations into victories simply by entering the thick of battle, riding high on his horse. Washington rallied and inspired his scattered forces to fight instead of retreat. At the battle of Princeton in 1777, Washington rode in front of his troops to encourage them, exposing himself to great personal danger. At one point during the battle Washington was caught in the crossfire between the two armies. One of the officers pulled his hat over his eyes to avoid seeing his general fall. But miraculously, when he looked again after the dust had settled, he saw that General Washington was unhurt, still high on his horse.

Hardships of War

General Washington struggled to overcome many difficulties during the long war. Although he had seen the British army in action and learned from it, he had not been formally trained in the art of European warfare. The British had a professional army whose troops were superior in numbers, military training, and discipline.

Without enough trained soldiers and supplies to fight an aggressive war, Washington's strategy was to conduct a defensive war. He avoided direct confrontation with British forces whenever necessary and used "hit and run" tactics. He also became successful in withdrawing by night, also called tactical retreat. Because of those tactics, some accused Washington of being too cautious. But he understood that final success would be achieved only if he avoided destruction of his army.

Many of Washington's difficulties came from the fact his duties were more extensive than those of a military leader today. Not only was he responsible for leading the fight, he recruited soldiers, purchased supplies and weapons, and did other administrative functions now done by staff. General Washington was an administrator as much as a fighter. He also had to keep thirteen governors happy with his actions. This was difficult, although it provided him with valuable training in diplomacy.

From the beginning, the Continental Army was troubled by hardships of inadequate arms and too little ammunition, provisions, and money. The pay was poor and infrequent. At the end of the war, some soldiers were still waiting for backpay. The army had no uniforms, and the men considered themselves lucky if they had worn-out clothes and shoes. Food was not only expensive but also in short supply. As the war lingered on, it brought hunger to the troops and much of the population.

As the Continental Army moved throughout the countryside, soldiers took what food they could find. They emptied barns and storehouses and stripped fields of crops, making farmers angry. Washington disapproved of the behavior and ordered his troops to pay farmers for any food they took.

In November 1777, the Continental Congress adopted the Articles of Confederation as the plan to govern the new nation. The Articles designated the United States of America as a "firm league of friendship" among thirteen independent states. The main governing body of the United States was the

Continental Congress—which had the power to set up a common defense, conduct foreign relations, and declare war. Congress alone was the unifying government of the thirteen states. There was no executive branch, and most of the judicial powers were given to states.

Yet, the Continental Congress found that it could not provide all the supplies desperately needed by the army. As a result it gave Washington new, unlimited powers to seize supplies. General Washington did not abuse the emergency powers given to him by Congress. In one of his most significant acts of leadership, Washington wisely refused to use such powers often. He believed the long-term effects of seizures to be more damaging than the short-term solutions they provided. Washington explained:

> Such procedures may give a momentary relief, but if repeated, will prove of the most pernicious consequence. Beside spreading disaffection, jealousy and fear in the people, they never fail, even in the most veteran troops, under the most rigid and exact discipline, to raise in the soldiery a disposition to licentiousness, plunder and robbery, difficult to suppress afterward, and which has proved not only ruinous to the inhabitants, but in many instances to armies themselves. I regret the occasion that compelled us to the measure the other day, and shall consider it among the greatest of our misfortunes, if we should be under the necessity of practicing it again.[57]

General Washington's vision of the Continental Army was that of a force serving its country, not one that ruled over it. He saw the army as the guarantor of liberty, not a means of tyranny. In the eighteenth century, that was a revolutionary idea in itself. Once again Washington demonstrated his motives—liberty for his country, not personal gain. In refusing unlimited power, Washington set the example of an ideal military leader.

Military discipline was crucial for success in the battlefield. To that end, Washington worked to protect his troops from the immoral influences of camp life. Washington was surprised "that the foolish, and wicked practice, of profane cursing and swearing (a vice heretofore little known in an American Army) is growing into fashion...it is a vice so mean and low without any temptation, that every man of sense, and character detests and despises it."[58] He ordered his generals to "Let vice and immorality of every kind be discouraged as much as possible in your brigade, and, as a chaplain is allowed to each regiment, see that the men regularly attend divine worship."[59]

Disease was also a big problem for the troops. The lack of sanitation, little or spoiled food, and crowded living quarters made the military camps vulnerable to all kinds of disease. This problem was so great that during the war more soldiers probably died of disease than in the battlefield.

In the winter of 1777-78, General Washington set up quarters in the village of Valley Forge, Pennsylvania. This was one of the most difficult times for the troops because they were hungry and cold. Most of their clothes were so worn they were in tatters. Some soldiers had to walk barefoot in the snow, bleeding with each step they took. To protect themselves from the bitter cold, the soldiers cut down trees and constructed huts. Miraculously Washington and the Continental Army survived the winter.

Washington often complained to Congress that his men suffered because they did not have blankets and clothes. Once, to make his point, he explained that 2,898 men were "now in camp unfit for duty because they are barefoot and otherwise naked."[60]

Washington blamed the Continental Congress for the extreme hardships experienced by his troops. He also complained of the character of some congressmen in whom "idleness, dissipation and extravagance seem to have laid fast hold of most of them...That party disputes and personal quarrels are the great business of the day...while the concerns of the nation are secondary."[61] The contrast between his poor, long-suffering troops and the wasteful members of Congress who did not supply the necessary provisions greatly upset him. Washington himself had made great personal sacrifices for his country, and he expected others to behave honorably. In spite of insufficient support from Congress, Washington obeyed the Congress throughout the war and thus established the principle of civilian control of the military.

For Washington, the troubles of war lessened when his wife Martha visited the camp. Martha Washington joined her husband whenever the fighting stopped and the army went into winter quarters. She usually stayed until spring when the fighting resumed. The troops called her Lady Washington, and her presence helped not only her husband but also boosted the soldiers' spirits. While there, her favorite activities included knitting socks for the troops and visiting the sick and wounded soldiers.

Washington's Critics

Washington often appealed to Congress for men, supplies, and money. However, he believed Congress interfered too much in military matters without providing enough help. For example, in a 1776 letter to his cousin Lund Washington, he complained that Congress did not want a regular army, preferring short-term enlistments instead. Washington wanted a regular army with trained soldiers who would serve for several years. With great discouragement, he wrote, "In confidence I tell you that I never was in such an unhappy, divided state since I was born."[62]

Although Washington was greatly admired by most people, even he had critics. Some talked of replacing him as commander-in-chief, because he had more defeats than victories in the beginning of the war. In fact, a few in Congress considered him insufficient as military leader and worked to weaken his authority. In addition, a rivalry existed between Washington and several generals who believed themselves better qualified to lead the army. When Washington made tactical errors, it gave his critics in Congress and among the generals ammunition to attack him.

Some of his critics even conspired against him. The best known conspiracy against Washington was known as the Conway Cabal, which took place in the winter of 1777-78, after the retreats at Brandywine and Germantown. A cabal is a secret group of political conspirators who try to undermine the power of a leader and assume it for themselves.

In October 1777, at Saratoga, New York, the American forces had won their greatest victory to date against the British. The general in charge was Horatio Gates, and his victory gave him hope of taking Washington's place as leader. General Thomas Conway, one of Gate's conspirators, had been a colonel in the French army before joining the American army. He had been trained in European warfare, had fought in European wars, and considered himself more experienced than any other American officer. He longed to be promoted to a major general, ahead of other American officers. Although Washington opposed it, Congress promoted Conway anyway.

Some letters between Conway and Gates, criticizing Washington's leadership, were considered conspiratorial. Even in Congress, a few seemed to favor removing Washington as commander-in-chief. Yet when it became known that Conway wrote insulting letters about Washington, the army rallied to support their general. Rumors flew that Washington had been insulted and that an effort was underway to get his resignation. American officers already upset at Congress for promoting Conway ahead of them wrote to Congress to complain. Seeing the extent of

Washington's support, even his critics in Congress changed their views and rallied around him. The Conway Cabal failed not only to remove Washington, but also showed people how indispensable he was to the war.

Keeping the Continental Army united despite a superior enemy, lack of resources, and attacks on his leadership, was one of the miracles of the Revolution. It was one of General Washington's greatest accomplishments.

Foreign Assistance

As the struggle for independence became known abroad, many foreign officers came to America's shores to help. Although most of them did not speak English, many expected high positions in the Continental Army, creating problems for Washington. Many were adventurers seeking to make their military reputations in the war, yet some made real contributions. Among them was Baron Friedrich von Steuben, a former Prussian officer who took over the training of the American troops at Valley Forge. He was a good drillmaster who taught the soldiers how to maneuver in ranks and how to use bayonets.

The best known of the foreign officers was the rich and influential French nobleman, the Marquis de Lafayette. Only nineteen years old in 1777 when he came to America to fight in the Revolution, the young marquis soon became Washington's friend and a strong supporter of the American cause to the French court.

Lafayette favored and promoted the military alliance between the French king and the United States, signed in February 1778. As a result of the alliance, the French provided troops and naval forces strong enough to stand against the powerful British fleet. Washington recognized that French assistance was essential to the American victory and was grateful for Lafayette's help. Without the French naval blockade during the battle of Yorktown, the Americans might not have won the war for independence.

Farewell and Resignation

The American victory at Yorktown, Virginia, in 1781 signaled the end of the Revolutionary War. Outnumbered by the American and French forces, the British General Cornwallis surrendered. Although the British surrendered in October 1781, the final peace treaty came later in September 1783, after a few more skirmishes on the western frontier.

On June 8, 1783, Washington wrote a letter to all the state governors as a farewell to public life. He asked them to read it to their legislatures. In the letter, Washington said that the people of the United States had a choice between being a "respectable and prosperous, or contemptible and miserable" nation. His advice focused on four areas he believed essential to the existence and prosperity of the new nation:

> 1st. An indissoluble union of the States under one federal head. 2dly. A sacred regard to public justice. 3dly. The adoption of a proper peace establishment, and 4thly. The prevalence of that pacific and friendly disposition, among the people of the United States, which will induce them to forget their local prejudices and policies, to make those mutual concessions which are requisite to the general prosperity, and in some instances, to sacrifice their individual advantages to the interest of the community.[63]

Washington's letter to the states emphasized his second point most of all. As commander-in-chief he felt it was his right to ask the governors to be just to the veterans of the war and provide the promised backpay. In his third point, he asked for establishment of a defense force. He explained, the militia of the Union "must be considered as a palladium of our security, and the first effectual resort in case of hostility."[64]

Washington ended his letter by asking Americans "to do justice, to love mercy, and to demean ourselves with that charity, humility, and pacific temper of mind, which were the characteristics of the Divine Author of our blessed religion, and without an humble imitation of whose example in these things, we can never hope to be a happy nation."[65]

After the peace treaty was signed, Washington disbanded the Continental Army and said an emotional farewell to his officers in New York. Then he traveled to Annapolis, Maryland, where Congress was meeting and formally resigned his commission.

For eight and a half years, Washington held more power than any other man in America. But when the war was over, he surrendered all that power willingly, and returned home. A victorious general giving up his power voluntarily was very unusual in the eighteenth century. That was a time when popular generals often became tyrants, but Washington did not use his personal popularity to hold on to power. That was part of his greatness, and the American people appreciated it.

Part Four

Statesman and President

Chapter 11

A Short Retirement

After more than eight years of the Revolutionary War, George Washington returned home to Mount Vernon on Christmas Eve, 1783. He was almost fifty-two years old when he retired from military service.

As the greatest hero of the war, Washington became the biggest celebrity of his time. People immortalized him in poems and pamphlets, and the trend to idolize him grew fast. His birthday became the country's first national day of celebration. Yet Washington himself was often embarrassed by the attention.

The price of fame was high. Daily he entertained an endless stream of visitors to Mount Vernon. He also responded to numerous fan letters and requests for portraits. In the days before photography was invented, a hand-painted portrait was the best way to have a picture of a hero. Since these portraits took a while to paint, Washington was forced to spend time posing for painters. He often complained of having to sit "like patience on a monument whilst they are delineating the lines of my face."[66] In time, he took it all in stride, but even then he never enjoyed it. He only endured it.

The Potomac River Company

During the five years between the end of the war and his election to the presidency, Washington served as president of the Potomac River Company. The company was created to improve navigation of the upper Potomac River and link it with the Ohio River. The states of Virginia and Maryland shared navigation rights to the Potomac River. Both state legislatures had approved the creation of a private company to develop the river and construct canals. Its long-term goal was to develop inland navigation through a network of canals. Some of those canals would connect future states in the west with the original Atlantic states, increasing trade and speeding up settlement of western lands.

Since the Potomac River flows by Mount Vernon, it was natural for George Washington to become involved. Washington had a vision for westward expansion of the United States even before it became a popular national goal.

The Constitution

From 1781 to 1788, the new nation was governed by a document called the Articles of Confederation. It was America's first, yet short-lived, constitution. Created in the midst of war, the Articles outlined a loose union of the thirteen states. Designed to protect America from tyranny, it established a Congress made up of delegates appointed by their state assemblies. It did not call for a president or a national judicial system, only the leaders of a weak Congress.

After the Revolution, the former colonies, now states, soon turned back to their independent ways. They exploited the weakness of the new government by defying many of its decisions. Although Congress had the power to make war, negotiate peace, and conduct foreign relations, it was not authorized to raise taxes or regulate commerce.

With a weak national government and no common enemy, each state focused on its own interests. Soon states even refused to cooperate with each other or respond to congressional requests. Because Congress had no power to control commerce, the states began to establish conflicting and confusing laws on tariffs and navigation. The loose Confederation of states was fast becoming unable to conduct critical business necessary for its survival. It could not pay war debts or coordinate a national defense. The fragile union was in danger of coming apart.

Washington also feared that such a weak union would make it possible for European powers to conquer the new country. In 1785, he wrote that

> local pursuits, and absurd jealousy are continually leading us from those great & fundamental principles which are characteristic of wise and powerful nations; and without which, we are no more than a rope of sand, and shall as easily be broken.[67]

He even wondered whether the new nation could succeed, "Is it possible after this that it should founder? Will not the all wise, & all powerful director of human events, preserve it?"[68] It was a crisis that had to be solved.

Other state leaders saw the same dangers of a weak union. In March 1785, representatives from Maryland and Virginia, the two states bordering the Potomac River, met to talk about their common commercial interests. The following year, Virginia invited all thirteen states to a convention. Although representatives from only five states attended the meeting, it was an important event because it showed that effective coordination among states would need significant national changes. The meeting ended with a call for a Constitutional Convention to meet in Philadelphia to revise the Articles of Confederation.

In May 1787, Washington attended the Constitutional Convention in Philadelphia as a delegate from Virginia. The convention lasted four months, from May 25 to September 17. During that time, delegates talked about the need to strengthen the new federal government by replacing the inadequate Articles of Confederation. Washington was elected president of the Constitutional Convention, lending his enormous prestige to the decisions made there.

In writing the Constitution, members of the Convention designed the presidency with George Washington in mind. Since they believed he would serve as the nation's first President, they gave the executive branch a great deal of power. They trusted Washington not to abuse it.

Three brilliant delegates—James Madison, Alexander Hamilton, and John Jay—wrote 85 articles, known as the Federalist Papers. In those articles they argued in favor of a strong federal government with an effective executive branch. After months of debate, America had a new document to govern its affairs—the Constitution.

The Federalists, who lived mainly in the commercial centers of the North, fought hard to ratify the Constitution. The Anti-Federalists resisted ratification because they favored strong state governments and a weak national government. They feared the Constitution would establish a strong federal government and give too much power to the president. The Anti-Federalists supported states' rights and wanted a system with little or no national government, no army, almost no central administration, and very restricted powers for the president.

Once the Constitution was drafted, the two factions were very active in promoting or opposing it. Its ratification was in question. Partisan politics had begun.

The Constitution could become the law of the land only after two-thirds of the states approved it through specially elected conventions. However, not all Americans desired a stronger central government. The Constitution's approval was not assured.

Following nine months of heated debate, the Constitution was formally adopted on June 21, 1788, after nine states ratified it. Washington's prestige helped ratify the Constitution, even by states fearful of a central government. After its ratification, Washington happily wrote to a friend:

> we may, with a kind of grateful and pious exultation, trace the finger of Providence through those dark and mysterious events, which first induced the States to appoint a general convention and then led them one after another (by such steps as were best calculated to effect the object) into an adoption of the system recommended by the general Convention.[69]

The Constitution is the highest law under which the United States government operates. It protects the rights of people against oppression and provides a framework for governing. The Constitution also separates powers among three branches of federal government: legislative, executive, and judicial. The legislative branch is the law-making body, known as the Congress. The executive branch, consisting of the President and executive departments, is the law enforcing body. The judicial branch is the law interpreting body, known as the Supreme Court. This separation of powers ensures that the government serves the people and does not oppress them.

George Washington had high expectations of the new government ruled by the Constitution. He wrote that it was his "most earnest wish that none but the most disinterested, able and virtuous men may be appointed to either house of Congress: because, I think, the tranquillity and happiness of this country will depend essentially upon that circumstance."[70]

Chapter 12

America's First President

George Washington was the obvious candidate for President of the United States. He was the only one who was well known, respected, and trusted in all thirteen states. No one had a national stature comparable with his. This was said to Washington by many people, including Benjamin Lincoln (a general during the Revolution):

> The share your Excellency holds in the affections of the people, and the unlimited confidence they place in your integrity and judgment, gives you an elevated stand among them which no other man can or probably ever will command.[71]

Washington, however, was reluctant to return to public life. He considered the call to the presidency as a bit of a misfortune. "For the great Searcher of human hearts knows there is no wish in mine, beyond that of living and dying an honest man, on my own farm."[72]

Sadly, Washington's health was also part of his reluctance. He was beginning to suffer from rheumatism. He wrote that the pain was sometimes so bad that he had a hard time raising his hand to his head or turning in bed. He also realized that being president involved a personal risk. What if the new system was not successful? This could ruin his reputation, something he valued highly.

With those reservations in mind, Washington did not campaign to be president. However, on February 4, 1789, the electoral college unanimously elected him as the first President of the United States.

Since communication was slow in the eighteenth century, Washington did not hear about his election until about two weeks later through a friend's letter. After receiving his official notice in April, Washington gave a modest response:

> I am so much affected by this fresh proof of my country's esteem and confidence, that silence can best explain my gratitude. While I realize the arduous nature of the task which is conferred on me and feel my inability to perform it, I wish there may not be reason for regretting the choice. All I can promise is only that which can be accomplished by an honest zeal.[73]

To his old comrade in arms, General Henry Knox, he wrote he was hesitant about leaving a peaceful private life "for an ocean of difficulties" and said "Integrity & firmness is all I can promise."[74]

Washington was fifty-seven years old when he left Mount Vernon for New York City, which was then the nation's capital. He assumed the presidency at the height of his fame and popularity. He had the public's affection and respect, as well as international prestige.

Inauguration

All along the way to his inauguration in New York, crowds enthusiastically welcomed their new president. There were many public celebrations, parades, banquets, and speeches.

At his first stop in Alexandria, a city near Mount Vernon, he said his "conviction of duty" compelled him to accept the presidency. Unlike politicians today, he did not make numerous promises. To the people of Alexandria, he said that as his neighbors they knew him well; he believed his life and past conduct spoke louder than any words. "The whole tenor of my life has been open to your inspection; and my past actions, rather than my present declarations, must be the pledge of my future conduct."[75]

Stopping to speak in Baltimore, he pledged that "no fear of encountering difficulties and no dread of losing popularity, shall ever deter me from pursuing what I conceive to be the true interests of my country."[76] He kept his pledge, even when it made him less popular.

On April 30, 1789, for the nation's first inauguration of a president, the city of New York was in a festive mood. Although a small city, with a population of only about 35,000 people, New York was full of flags and colorful decorations. The people celebrated, and hung wreaths and flowers from their windows.

When George Washington arrived at Federal Hall, all eyes were upon him. He was dressed in a dark brown suit with medal buttons decorated with eagles, and a sword at his side. Washington took the oath of office on the balcony of the Senate Chamber, and then bowed to kiss the Bible. Back inside the Senate Chamber he read his Inaugural Address, but he was so moved that his hands trembled as he held the paper. In his Inaugural Address, he pledged to pursue the public good and not be influenced by local prejudices, attachments, or partisan quarrels. He added "that the foundations of our national policy, will be laid in the pure and immutable principles of private morality."[77] A substantial part of his Inaugural Address pointed to God's role in the affairs of the nation:

it would be peculiarly improper to omit in this first official act, my fervent supplications to that Almighty Being who rules over the universe, who presides in the councils of nations,....that his benediction may consecrate to the liberties and happiness of the people of the United States....No people can be bound to acknowledge and adore the invisible hand, which conducts the affairs of men more than the people of the United States. Every step, by which they have advanced to the character of an independent nation, seems to have been distinguished by some token of providential agency.[78]

Founding a Nation

Just as Washington rose to the challenge of winning a Revolution, he also rose to face an equally difficult challenge of founding a nation. The United States was a new experiment in self-government. Many doubted it would last.

Washington had presided over a complicated transformation of the country from a loose and weak confederation of states to a union. He then took charge of a new government with no history or examples to follow, and led the country during its difficult formative years.

Washington practically invented the office and the role of the president. The office benefited greatly from his dignity, and soon he left his permanent mark on the institution.

Without the unity created by a British king, President Washington became the bond and point of common reference for all Americans. For many former British citizens, Washington was replacing the king who had once ruled. Even

President Washington at his inauguration in New York.

though some people talked about making him king, he did not even consider it.

Although Washington had little experience in civil administration, he was a hands-on president. Knowing the previous system of government had failed, he wanted the new union and its federal government to succeed. He had supported the new Constitution, and as president he was going to make it work.

President Washington faced critical issues, such as inflation and domestic and foreign debts from the Revolutionary War. He also needed to establish a national defense. In addition, he needed to establish diplomatic relations with other nations, develop a legal system, and establish weights and measures. The new nation also had to have a uniform currency and financial union of all the states.

President Washington led the nation forward. He advanced the nation's commerce, agriculture, and manufacturing capabilities. He presided over establishment of important institutions, such as the federal courts and the executive branch.

Many debates had occurred in Congress over the bills establishing the executive departments of war, treasury, and state because the president would be given power to remove the heads of those departments. In the end, however, Congress approved the bills and gave the president powers to appoint and remove the heads of executive departments.

One issue dear to Washington's heart was that of an American national identity. The population of the United States, nearly four million strong, did not have a national consciousness or identity. As president, Washington campaigned hard to establish a national identity and eliminate regional jealousies.

Washington believed the president should stay above partisan politics. During his first term, he avoided personal promotion of issues and did not get involved in congressional legislation.

Without political parties in the first presidential election, the candidate with the second largest number of votes became vice president. Hence John Adams of Massachusetts became the first vice president of the United States. The two men had worked well together during the Revolutionary War when Adams was a prominent member of Congress. However, they were not friends. During Washington's presidency, they did not work closely together, partly due to Adams' envy of Washington's fame and popularity. The chilled relations resulted in a trivial role for the vice president, setting a pattern that continues today.

Washington understood he was setting precedents, and he took care to establish right principles. He wrote to Vice President Adams:

> Many things which appear of little importance in themselves...may have great and durable consequences from their having been established at the commencement of a new general government.[79]

Washington was deeply aware that he walked "on untrodden ground...There is scarcely any part of my conduct which may not hereafter be drawn into precedent."[80]

In 1789, at Congress' direction, Washington issued the first presidential Thanksgiving Proclamation. Thursday, the 26th of November, was proclaimed a day of public thanksgiving to give thanks to "that great and glorious Being, who is the beneficent Author of all the good that was, that is, or that will be."[81] It was a day of prayer with thanksgiving for past blessings, as well as regret over national transgressions. It was not the four-day holiday it is today.

During Washington's second year as president, the nation's capital was moved from New York to Philadelphia. Philadelphia has a population over 60,000 when it became the capital. Yet it was only temporary until a permanent capital was found. In September 1790, Congress approved a permanent capital to be built between Maryland and Virginia on the banks of the Potomac River, in a land now known as the District of Columbia.

President Washington approved of a decision to place the new capital on the banks of the Potomac River. He was most interested in its design. The "Federal City," as it was called then, was later named in Washington's honor, although he would not live to see it finished.

Illnesses

Twice during his presidency, Washington became seriously ill. During his first year as president, in June 1789, Washington developed a large swelling on his left thigh that produced an abscess and severe fever. He needed surgery, but eighteenth-century medicine was primitive. Surgery was risky, especially because of the possibility of infection. However, President Washington recovered completely several weeks after surgery, again demonstrating his hardy constitution and overcoming spirit.

Then, in May 1790, President Washington became ill with influenza, an epidemic spreading quickly through New York causing many deaths. Again, many feared he would die. People were so concerned about his illness they laid straw on the street in front of the presidential house to dull the noise of passing carriages so he could rest and recover.

Jefferson wrote a friend describing the great public alarm regarding Washington's fate:

> we have been very near losing the President. He was taken with a peripneumony and on the 5th day he was pronounced by two of the three physicians present to be in the act of death...You cannot conceive the public alarm on this occasion. It proves how much depends on his life.[82]

Again, Washington miraculously recovered and went on with the task of governing. He wrote he was pleased with the new government and that "though not absolutely perfect, is one of the best in the world."[83]

Washington's Cabinet

For his first administration, Washington selected some of the most brilliant Americans of his time. Among them were John Jay, the Chief Justice; Alexander Hamilton, the Secretary of the Treasury; Thomas Jefferson, the Secretary of State; Edmund Randolph, the Attorney General; and General Knox, the Secretary of War. Washington did not limit them to their department's specialty, but considered them general advisors. President Washington asked for advice from many people; it was not his way to simply wield power.

The men who served in President Washington's cabinet did not agree on everything. In fact, there was much disagreement. For example, Hamilton and Jefferson at times were on such opposite sides on issues that not even Washington could reconcile them.

Jefferson, a Southerner from Virginia, and Hamilton, an Easterner from New York, disagreed over most policy issues. Jefferson was an advocate for state rights. He saw the United States as an agricultural nation. Hamilton was an advocate for a strong federal government and a national bank. He supported commerce and manufacturing as the nation's future. The two men mirrored the regional conflicts of their day.

Both Hamilton and Jefferson respected Washington and wanted his approval. Hamilton had gained Washington's trust and friendship during the Revolutionary War. He became a dominant figure during his first administration. Like Washington, Jefferson was a farmer and a Virginian.

Yet Washington understood that in order to prosper, the United States must have an economy that involved manufacturing and commerce, not just agriculture.

Although he would not have called himself a "Federalist," President Washington supported many Federalist ideals. In fact, when both Hamilton and Jefferson resigned, Washington's Cabinet was made up entirely of Federalist men. But Washington was very much against political parties and thus never became a Federalist.

Chapter 13

Second Term

By the end of his first four-year term, President Washington longed to retire. He said he felt old and complained about a weakening memory. Yet he was still indispensable to the new nation, as Thomas Jefferson wrote:

> The confidence of the whole union is centered in you. Your being at the helm, will be more than an answer to every argument which can be used to alarm and lead the people in any quarter into violence or secession. North and South will hang together, if they have you to hang on.[84]

That is why, he sacrificed his own desires for retirement, and was persuaded by Alexander Hamilton and Jefferson to stay for a second term.

On February 13, 1793, Washington was unanimously re-elected as president. Once again, he did not campaign. He simply did not refuse re-election, which was taken to mean he accepted. President Washington's second Inaugural Address on March 4, 1793, the shortest one to date, was only 135 words.

After his Inauguration, Washington went home and gave $150 to the poor, a large sum of money at that time.

Since he did not believe in boasting, it is not surprising he did it quietly. His account books show that he often gave to charity.

The French Revolution

President Washington believed strongly that unity and a common purpose were essential for the American government and its citizens. Yet those ideals were to be severely tested during his second term.

During that time, problems in Europe were having major effects on American politics. The French Revolution divided the American public, as well as Washington's cabinet. Many Americans, including Jefferson, believed the French Revolution was much like the American Revolution. They continued to support it, even after its excesses and violence became known.

However, Washington continued to be cautious about forming alliances. He wanted to avoid any military involvement with France. In 1793, France declared war against Britain. France then attempted to pull the United States into the war by invoking a treaty negotiated during the American Revolution between the king of France and the United States. However, France had executed the king, and Washington thought it strange the French would bring it up.

Although many Americans supported the French Revolution, Washington considered peace essential for building a great nation. In April 1793, against the advice of some in his cabinet, as well as public opinion, Washington refused to get involved and declared neutrality, risking his own popularity. He based the decision on his convictions of what was good for the country, not on short-term popular opinion.

History proved that neutrality was the best course, although it damaged Washington's reputation and popularity for a while. People would surround his presidential house and demand he help the French by starting a war against England. The anti-Federalist press bitterly attacked him and his policies. Not used to such criticism, he did not take it well. Jefferson wrote that in response to criticism Washington had an unusual outburst of temper:

> the President was much inflamed...Defied any man on earth to produce one single act of his since he had been in the government which was not done on the purest motives...That by god he had rather be in his grave than in his present situation. That he had rather be on his farm than to be made emperor of the world.[85]

Jay's Treaty

Another difficult issue during Washington's second term was the new treaty with Britain, popularly known as Jay's Treaty. Under the earlier 1783 peace treaty that ended the American Revolution, the British agreed to surrender their inland forts. Later, however, they refused to leave them until the United States carried out its agreement to compensate the Loyalists for lost property.

In addition, the British were seizing American merchant ships to prevent them from taking food and supplies to the French. To address those problems, Washington sent a special envoy to London in 1794. He chose a man he trusted, John Jay, the chief justice of the Supreme Court, to negotiate a new treaty with Britain.

In the new treaty Britain again agreed to leave its military posts on the frontier, as well as pay for the seized American ships. But the treaty did not include British compensation for the Southern slaves it had freed during the war.

Although President Washington was disappointed with the treaty, he supported it, because it was the best possible deal for a powerless new nation. It also kept peace with Britain. However, many Americans were against Jay's Treaty because they felt it did not accomplish enough. Many were upset because the treaty said the United States still had to pay debts owed to British merchants for pre-Revolutionary accounts.

It was not easy for Washington to persuade the Senate to ratify the treaty, or for the House to provide funds for its enforcement. Both Britain and France had friends in the United States who sought to influence the nation's policy. Many people supported or opposed the treaty based only on whether they were pro-French or pro-British.

President Washington's neutrality in France's war with Britain and his support of Jay's Treaty earned him much criticism and abuse. Yet within several months, the majority of people began to accept the treaty. Jefferson, who was pro-French, wrote a friend about Washington's influence: "Such is the popularity of the President, that the people will support him in whatever he will or will not do, without appealing to their own reason or to anything but their feelings toward him."[86]

The Farewell Address

Washington's famous Farewell Address to the nation was not a speech. It was printed in September 1796, as a 6,000-word article in newspapers across the country. Through it, Washington told the American people that he would not accept a third term, and he thanked the nation for the many honors it had given him.

The lasting legacy of the Farewell Address lies in the wise advice Washington gave to his beloved country. Called Washington's political testament, the Farewell Address is considered one of the major contributions to American political thought.

In his Farewell Address, Washington first addressed the importance of the American union and the evils of regional and other factionalism, including political parties. "The name of AMERICAN, which belongs to you, in your national capacity, must always exalt the just pride of patriotism, more than any appellation derived from local discriminations."[87] The United States was still very young when Washington left office, and he saw a critical need for the new nation to have a national identity if it was to survive and succeed.

Second, Washington emphasized the need for religion and morality in government. "Of all the dispositions and habits which lead to political prosperity, religion and morality are indispensable supports....reason and experience both forbid us to expect that national morality can prevail in exclusion of religious principle."[88]

Third, Washington talked about foreign relations and his doctrine of national self-interest. "Observe good faith and justice towards all nations. Cultivate peace and harmony with all."[89] Yet, he warned against foreign influence. "The nation, which indulges towards another an habitual hatred, or an habitual fondness, is in some degree a slave. It is a slave to its animosity or to its affection, either of which is sufficient to lead it astray from its duty and its interest."[90] Washington advocated his own policy "to steer clear of permanent alliances" and to "safely trust to temporary alliances for extraordinary emergencies."[91]

Washington could have remained President until his death. However, he stepped down to allow the citizens to choose their next president, setting another vital precedent in American history. In a young republic that could have failed easily, Washington was truly the essential ingredient that brought success.

At the end of his presidency, Washington left a legacy of remarkable accomplishments. He had risked everything to lead the Revolutionary War. Facing the world's greatest military power, Washington avoided defeat of an ill-equipped army to win a revolution. Steering a new nation through a troubled first decade, he had left his mark on the Office of the President. He protected the fragile union from getting mixed up in foreign wars. He established a balanced system of governing. A man who understood and used power wisely, Washington established an orderly transfer of power. Washington's great legacy also included his exceptional personal example of leadership.

Chapter 14

Retirement

At age sixty-five, George Washington retired from public life at last. He planned to live a quiet life on his farms, although he had been in public life far too long not to care about what was going on in America and the world. Mount Vernon was far from the center of power, but Washington was not isolated. Through letters he kept in touch with many people, including members of President Adams' cabinet.

Washington's daily routine at Mount Vernon included tours of his farms on horseback. He would begin his inspections after an early breakfast and return in time for an early dinner around two o'clock. At dinner, he would always entertain visitors, including strangers, who came to pay their respects. He had become not only the patriarch of his own family, but of the whole nation.

Brief Recall to Service

In the summer of 1798, his retirement was interrupted one last time by a call from the new President, John Adams. In response to American negotiations with the British, the

French had raided American ships and refused to accept American diplomats in Paris. Fearing a French invasion, President Adams prepared for war and asked Washington to take command of the army again.

In November 1798, Washington returned to Philadelphia for five weeks to make plans for recruiting and supplying an army. For several months he led preparations for war. Fortunately, the dispute with France was resolved peacefully, and Washington was able to return to his retirement.

A Hero's Death

Washington's death came unexpectedly. On December 12, 1799, he was touring his farms on horseback for about five hours. During that time, it began snowing. Then a cold rain fell while he was on his way home. That evening, it became clear he had a cold. The next day he stayed inside because of a severe sore throat. He spoke with a hoarseness that worsened until evening. During the night, he became seriously ill and had difficulty breathing. While he told Martha he was ill around three o'clock, he would not let her get out of bed to call a servant because he did not want her to catch a cold in the freezing night air. In the morning, a worker on his farms was called to come and bleed him. Bleeding was a common medical practice in the eighteenth century.

His old friend Dr. James Craik from Alexandria came in the morning. Dr. Craik diagnosed Washington as having an inflammation of the throat. He gave him the standard medications of that time including a mixture of vinegar and water vapors, and more bleedings.

Dr. Craik consulted with two other doctors who arrived that afternoon. The three of them did everything they could to save Washington. Unfortunately, nothing they did helped.

Washington realized he was dying. That afternoon he asked Martha to bring him the two wills from his desk. Then he asked her to burn one of them and put the other in a safe place. As the illness progressed, it became more painful for him to speak. He spent his last hours with his wife Martha, Tobias Lear his secretary and friend, and his old friend, Dr. Craik. Lawrence Lewis, one of Washington's favorite nephews who was living at Mount Vernon, had left on a trip a few days earlier and was not home.

On December 14, 1799, about ten o'clock at night, George Washington died. He was almost 68 years old.

A Nation Mourns

In his will, Washington said he wanted to have a small private funeral. However, people came from miles around to be at his funeral on December 18. The military, both cavalry and foot soldiers came from Alexandria to take part. Washington was laid to rest in the family vault on the grounds of Mount Vernon.

In Philadelphia, the nation's capital, Congress passed a resolution calling for people to wear black armbands for thirty days as a sign of mourning. It also arranged for a mock funeral procession to be held in the capital on December 26, 1799.

As news of his death spread around the country, many memorial services and numerous eulogies (formal statements of praise) were given. Congressman Henry Lee, who had been an officer in the Continental Army and knew Washington well, was given the honor of giving the nation's official eulogy. His words spoke most eloquently for a nation in deep mourning:

> First in war, first in peace, and first in the hearts of his countrymen, he was second to none in humble and

enduring scenes of private life. Pious, just, humane, temperate, and sincere; uniform, dignified, and commanding; his example was as edifying to all around him...Correct throughout, vice shuddered in his presence and virtue always felt his fostering hand. The purity of his private character gave effulgence to his public virtues...Such was the man for whom our nation mourns.[92]

References:

[1] Abbot, W. W., The Papers of George Washington, Colonial Series, vol. 1, (Charlottesville, University Press of Virginia, 1983), p. 226.

[2] Ibid, p. 343.

[3] Ibid, p. 107.

[4] Chastellux, Marquis de, (translation by Howard C. Rice Jr.), Travels in North America, vol. 1, (Chapel Hill, University of North Carolina Press, 1963), p. 114.

[5] Mitchell, Stewart, New Letters of Abigail Adams 1788-1801, (Boston, Houghton Mifflin Co., 1947), p. 15.

[6] Chase, Philander, The Papers of George Washington, Revolutionary War Series, vol. 1, (Charlottesville, University of Virginia, 1985), p. 4.

[7] Abbot, op. cit. , vol. 8, p. 90.

[8] Chase, op. cit., vol. 4, p. 485.

[9] Abbot, op. cit., Confederation Series, vol. 1, p. 123.

[10] Twohig, Dorothy, The Papers of George Washington, Presidential Series, vol. 4, (Charlottesville, University of Virginia, 1987), p. 32.

[11] Chastellux, op. cit, p. 113.

[12] Ibid, p. 114.

[13] Thane, Elswyth, Potomac Squire, (Mount Vernon, VA, Mt. Vernon Ladies' Association, 1963), pp. 281-2.

[14] Humphreys, David, (edited by Zagarri, Rosemarie) Life of General Washington, , (Athens, University of Georgia Press, 1991), pp. 53-54.

[15] Chase, op. cit., Revolutionary War Series, vol. 3, p. 528.

[16] Abbot, op. cit., Confederation Series, vol. 1, p. 439.

[17] Fitzpatrick, John, C., The Writings of George Washington, vol. 35, (Washington, DC, U.S. Government Printing Office, 1931-44), p. 422.

[18] Ibid, vol. 30, p. 67.

[19] Ibid, vol. 37, p. 95.

[20] Desmond, Alice, Curtis, George Washington's Mother, (New York, Dodd, Mead & Company, 1961), p. 91.

[21] Humphreys, op. cit., p. 56.

[22] Abbot, op. cit., Confederation Series, vol. 2, p. 29.

[23] Ibid, p. 175.

[24] Abbot, op. cit., Confederation Series, vol. 1, p. 258.

[25] Chase, op. cit., Revolutionary War Series, vol. 1, p. 4.

[26] Ibid, vol. 5, p. 246.

[27] Ibid, p. 155.

[28] Fitzpatrick, op, cit., vol. 12, p. 157.

[29] Ibid, p. 345.

[30] Abbot, op. cit., Confederation Series, vol .2, p. 473.

[31] Twohig, op., cit., Presidential Series, vol. 2, p. 174.

[32] Ibid, p. 412.

[33] Ibid, vol. 3, p. 497.

[34] Ibid, vol. 2 p. 424.

[35] Fitzpatrick, op. cit., vol. 31, p. 93.

[36] Twohig, op. cit., Presidential Series, vol. 4, p. 467.

[37] Ibid, vol. 2, p. 420.

[38] Fitzpatrick, op. cit., vol. 35, p. 229.

[39] Abbot, op. cit., Confederation Series, vol .3, p. 383.

[40] Ibid, vol .2, p. 184.

[41] Ibid, vol. 3, p. 84.

[42] Fitzpatrick, op. cit., vol. 26, p. 39.

[43] Abbot, op. cit., Confederation Series, vol. 3, p. 10.

[44] Ibid, p. 10.

[45] Andrust, Ralph, K. George Washington A Biography in His Own Words, (1972), p. 186.

[46] Ibid, pp. 242-3.

[47] Ibid, p. 244.

[48] Twohig, op. cit., Presidential Series, vol. 1, p. 438.

[49] Ibid, p. 439.

[50] Ibid, p. 439.

[51] Fitzpatrick, op. cit., vol. 26, p. 40.

[52] Chase, op. cit., Revolutionary War Series, vol. 1, p. 1.

[53] Ibid, vol. 2, p. 346.

[54] Ibid, vol. 3, p. 362.

[55] Ibid, pp. 24-5.

[56] Ibid, p. 569.

[57] Fitzpatrick, op. cit., vol. 10, p. 267.

[58] Chase, op. cit., Revolutionary War Series, vol. 5, p. 551

[59] Fitzpatrick, op. cit., vol. 8, p. 129.

[60] Ibid, vol. 10, p. 195.

[61] Chase, op. cit., Revolutionary War Series, vol. 9, p. 533

[62] Ibid, vol. 6, p. 441

[63] Fitzpatrick, op. cit., vol. 26, p. 487.

[64] Ibid, p. 494.

[65] Ibid, p. 496.

[66] Abbot, op. cit., Confederation Series, vol. 2, p. 561.

[67] Ibid, p. 400.

[68] Ibid, vol. 1, p. 385.

[69] Fitzpatrick, op. cit., vol. 30, p. 22.

[70] Twohig, op. cit., Presidential Series, vol. 1, p. 199.

[71] Twohig, op. cit., Presidential Series, vol. 1, p. 6.

[72] Ibid, p. 200.

[73] Ibid, vol. 2, p. 56.

[74] Ibid, p. 2.

[75] Ibid, p. 60.

[76] Ibid, p. 62.

[77] Ibid, p. 175.

[78] Ibid, p. 174.

[79] Ibid, pp. 246-7.

[80] Ibid, vol. 4, p. 552.

[81] Ibid, pp. 131-2.

[82] Boyd, Julian, P., (editor), The Papers of Thomas Jefferson, vol. 16, (Princeton University Press, 1961), p. 444.

[83] Twohig, op. cit., Presidential Series, vol. 4, p. 552.

[84] Boyd, op. cit., vol. 23, p. 539.

[85] Boyd, op. cit., vol. 26, pp. 602-603.

[86] Malone, Dumas, Jefferson and the Ordeal of Liberty, (Boston, Little, Brown and Company, 1962), p. 271.

[87] Fitzpatrick, op. cit., vol. 35, pp. 219-20.

[88] Ibid, p. 229.

[89] Ibid, p. 231.

[90] Ibid, p. 231.

[91] Ibid, pp. 234-5.

[92] Lee, Henry, A Funeral Oration, (Portsmouth, 1800) p. 10.

Appendix

Web Sites:

www.mountvernon.org -- information on George Washington and his home, Mount Vernon.

www.virginia.edu/gwpapers/ -- information on George Washington's letters and other writings.